GATHERED MEMORIES

Gathered ✕ ✕ Memories

(EASTERN STAR CEREMONIES)

Containing 30 programs for various occasions during the fraternal year

BY RUTH ADAMS (*Arizona*)
ETTA MAY GIBBANY (*Missouri*)
MARGARET MELISSINOS (*New York*)
CORNELIA SCHATMEYER (*New Jersey*)
DOROTHY TRIMBLE (*Indiana*)

Macoy Publishing and Masonic Supply Company, Inc.
RICHMOND, VIRGINIA

ISBN-0-88053-308-0

Library of Congress Catalog Card No. 61-15946

Printed in the United States of America

"Sweet thoughts can never die
Treasured and blessed—
God knows how deep they lie
Stored in the breast."

TABLE OF CONTENTS

CEREMONIES TO HONOR RETIRING
MATRON AND PATRON

1. Hawaii Calling
By Etta May Gibbany, P.M.
(Missouri)

⤙

A ceremony to honor the Retiring Worthy Matron and Worthy Patron or a District Deputy at the end of her year. If used for Deputy, change "Worthy Matron" to "Deputy," etc. The Conductress is the principal speaker.

CONDUCTRESS:

Worthy Matron,
We are happy tonight to welcome you,
Our honored guest, most loyal and true.
You carried the torch that turned night to day
As we walked together the star-lit way.

Worthy Patron,
Your leadership strong, your guidance, too—
Say you *also* are one to whom honor is due.
Lead by the Star, high service to attain,
Your year will shine brightly down Memory Lane.

SOLOIST: "Because You Came To Us"—*(Both W.M. & W.P. standing)*

(To be sung to the tune of "Because," popular wedding song.)

Because you came to us to serve with love,
And held our Eastern Star all else above,
Your year was filled with joy for all, and thus
We're glad you came to us!

Because your smile brought happy, golden hours
We found our pathway strewn with fragrant flowers,
And as you leave we vision ivory towers—
Because you came to us.

Because your loyalty we highly praise,
Through day and night, through spring and autumn
    days—
We'll pray His love will fill your life always,
Because you came to us!

CONDUCTRESS:

Worthy Matron and Worthy Patron,
    With your offices ended in Eastern Star,
    There is one decision you will probably face:
    Since holiday time is not very far
    You will wish to choose a vacation place.

Across the beautiful, mighty blue—
    Where adventure, relaxing and rest await—
    We hear Hawaii calling you
    To our new and fabulous fiftieth state!

The "spell of the islands" true gladness will render
    With gaiety and luxury, real beauty will entice—
    To the tropical verdure and scenic splendor
    Of this charming, "Pacific Paradise."

If you choose to travel on a speedy jetliner
Or on one of the great and luxurious ships—
We believe your holiday fun will be finer
If you follow some of our helpful trip tips.

ADAH:

If your holiday starts at Waikiki Beach
On the beautiful island of scenic Oahu—
I wish to present a lei to each.
To remind you of Adah, the flowers are blue!

(Here Adah presents a lei of blue to Worthy Matron &
Worthy Patron.)

RUTH:

And I have for each a yellow lei—
To remind you of the gleaner Ruth.
Do visit a Chapter on your way—
For there are our sisters and brothers in truth.

(Ruth presents a yellow lei to each of these officers)

ESTHER:

My leis are white for purity,
To recall Queen Esther's bravery.
Do see the Shriners' Hospital through
While touring the City of Hōnolulu.

(Esther presents each with a lei of white)

MARTHA:

When you see Pearl Harbor, though the view be brief,
And the National Cemetery in Punch Bowl crater—
You may recall Martha's sisterly grief,
But wonder if America's grief was greater.

(Martha presents each with a lei of green)

ELECTA:

My lei of red is a symbol of love,
And recalls Electa's loving deeds.
May help and guidance from above
Make safe your journey from all that impedes.

(Electa presents each with a lei of red, after which both will be seated.)

CONDUCTRESS:

Worthy Matron,

(Worthy Matron rises)

Now when you travel our tropical state
Sugar plantations and pineapple, too—
Will lure to a wonderland, luscious and great,
Revealing many a breath-taking view.

And as you may sit where Princess Kaiulani
Listened to Robert Louis Stevenson's lore
Worthy Matron, I proclaim you our "Pineapple Princess"
Who we shall always love and adore.

We can picture our Princess in a tropical garden
Very near to a shimmering, lazy lagoon,
With an exotic sunset, or—strumming ukuleles
Beneath a silvery, mellow moon!

NOTE: The above will be most effective if given from memory, while "Aloha Oe," (Farewell to Thee) is played softly as background music. With some practice, the rhythm of the words and music will fit together nicely.

Favors and decorations may be as elaborate as desired, to simulate Hawaiian scenes.

2. *Lighting Our Candles*

By Ruth Adams, P.M.

(Arizona)

﹏

Ceremony to honor Retiring Matron and Patron at last meeting of the year. To be given just before retiring march. The Sentinel may enter room after Chapter has been closed. Each officer speaks from her station.

———

A.M.:

Sister _____,

    Your year as Worthy Matron of _____ Chapter
    Has been filled with shining light,
    And we have shared with you this year
    In service—in truth—and in right.

    The light which you carried with you
    Served as a guide for us all,
    So tonight we've brought *our* lights
    To brighten up our Chapter room hall.

(Have lights dimmed as low as possible so that the candles will show more effectively. Candles for W.M. and W.P. may have their names on them. Safety candles are recommended or if burning candles are used it is suggested that aluminum foil be twisted around base of each to catch dripping and reflect light. A.M. and A.P. should have holders as they will have to set theirs on pedestals when they go to the East to present gifts. Each officer lights candle before speaking.)

CHAPLAIN:

>Sister _____,
>>One light you carried all through the year—
>>One light to inspire and guide you true,
>>And as a symbol of your one light
>>Is this candle of faith and prayer for you.

>>>*(gives candle)*

MARSHAL:

>Brother _____,
>>You also carried a light in your heart
>>That burned with a steadfast flame,
>>And as a symbol of your one true light
>>This candle of fraternal love bears your name.

>>>*(gives candle)*

WARDER:

>Sister _____ and Brother _____,
>>I light my candle of peace
>>In gratitude for a harmonious year
>>For you have guided our Chapter
>>By a light ever shining and clear.

ORGANIST:

>Sister _____ and Brother _____,
>>I light my candle of harmony
>>To represent the beauty of music and song,
>>For harmony has been with us all this year
>>As you lighted our way all along.

ASSOCIATE CONDUCTRESS:

Sister _____ and Brother _____,
I light my candle of good discipline
For such has been ours all this year,
And you have each been led by His Light
And worked day by day without fear.

CONDUCTRESS:

Sister _____ and Brother _____,
I light my candle of fulfillment
For it was a joy to tend the light,
Our plans have been very successful
And we've found joy in each meeting night.

CHAPLAIN:

Sister _____ and Brother _____,
I light my candle of devotion
For the Holy Bible has been our Light,
And it has been a great privilege
To kneel at the altar each meeting night.

MARSHAL:

Sister _____ and Brother _____,
I light my candle of direction
To represent courtesy and promptness, too,
For you inspire us by your leadership
To be kind and thoughtful in all we do.

A.M.:

Sister _____ and Brother _____,
I light my candle of light itself
To represent the sun so shining bright,
For you have been true to our teachings
And have filled our lives with light.

A.P.:

Sister _____ and Brother _____,
   I light my candle of divine guidance
   In appreciation of this year in the West,
   It has been a privilege to serve with you
   And our Chapter has been richly blessed.

TREASURER:

Sister _____ and Brother _____,
   I light my candle of security
   To say thanks for a prosperous year,
   Our lights have burned so brightly
   That our books are in the clear.

SECRETARY:

Sister _____ and Brother _____,
   I light my candle of intelligence
   As I say thanks for your kind deeds,
   My work has been made much easier
   For you've fulfilled all my needs.

SENTINEL:

Sister _____ and Brother _____,
   I light my candle of protection
   Just as I guarded the door with care,
   It has been a joy to greet many friends
   Who have visited us from everywhere.

ADAH:

Sister _____ and Brother _____,
   I light my blue candle of fidelity
   To say thanks for your kindliness,
   It has been a joy to share with you
   This year of light and happiness.

RUTH:

Sister _____ and Brother _____,
  I light my yellow candle of constancy
  To say thanks for adding much beauty,
  It has been a privilege to share with you
  This year of light and devotion to duty.

ESTHER:

Sister _____ and Brother _____,
  I light my white candle of loyalty
  To say thanks for your help in every task,
  It has been an honor to share with you
  As in the light and the joy we basked.

MARTHA:

Sister _____ and Brother _____,
  I light my green candle of faith and hope
  To say thanks for inspiring us anew,
  It has been a peaceful, happy time
  This year of light shining through.

ELECTA:

Sister _____ and Brother _____,
  I light my red candle of love and charity
  To say thanks for the love everywhere,
  It has been a year of fulfillment
  With light and love for all to share.

SOLOIST:

(May use favorite song of W.M. or change names of following to the tune of "Daisy, Daisy Give Me Your Answer True.")

_____, _____, _____ and _____, too,
We have lighted—our candles of love for you,
Your light will keep right on shining
And you won't be repining
You'll both be fine
Your light will shine
Just as bright as it shines tonight.

(A.M. and A.P. go to the East to make gift presentations)

A.M.:

Sister _____,

    You've carried your light of peace

    (may insert other motto for peace & harmony, etc.)

    And harmony has filled our hall,
    So tonight your officers join with me
    To say thanks from one and all.

    We have good wishes for your future
    And we hope the best comes to you,
    For we could search the wide world over
    And never find a Matron more true.

    I have the pleasant privilege
    Of presenting this gift to you tonight,
    From your nineteen *(year)* officers
    Who have helped you "tend the light."

A.P.:

Brother _____,

    Your pleasant smile and kindly manner
    Have made the members all love you
    For you've exemplified Masonic teachings
    In everything you set out to do.

We've good wishes too for you
In the years that are yet to be
For you've demonstrated fraternal love
In a manner kindly and free.

It is a very great pleasure for me
To present from your officers tonight
This gift of love and sincere thanks
For a year of harmony and shining light.

3. A Floral Farewell to the Retiring Matron & Patron

Optional: Signing the Altar Bible
By Margaret Melissinos
(New York)

〜

The Floral Staff, led by the Floral Matron and Patron, enter the room and take positions on the floor, the Floral Matron and Patron standing directly in front of the East.

The Floral Star Points carry flowers, each point carrying the color representing her station.

FLORAL MATRON:

Dear Worthy Matron and Worthy Patron, our tasks for you this year have all been enjoyable ones. The ceremony, this evening, is the exception. There are no joyous words that bid farewell, and yet we are comforted in knowing that when you take leave of your office, you will continue to meet with us.

FLORAL CONDUCTRESS:

Dear Worthy Matron and Worthy Patron, will you give us the honor of escorting you through the rays of the Star, whose brilliant colors glow especially for you tonight?

FLORAL ASSOC. CONDUCTRESS:

Soft words of farewell await you at each lovely point, and the beautiful symbol of our Order awaits your coming.

(Floral Conductress and Associate Conductress approach the East and escort the Matron and Patron of the Chapter to each point on the floor, beginning with Adah.)

ADAH:

>The point of Adah is quite blue;
>>Perhaps the thought of losing you
>Has helped its tone to grow more deep;
>>Oh, how this little flower must weep!

(Adah presents her flower to the Worthy Matron)

RUTH:

>As Ruth, my point of purest gold
>>Is in the flower that I hold;
>Its glow has bathed your 12-month stay
>>With highlights that reflect each ray.

(Ruth presents her flower to the Worthy Matron)

ESTHER:

>Queen Esther, with her lily white
>>Bids both of you farewell tonight;
>The pureness of this lovely one
>>Has graced each single thing you've done.

(Esther presents her flower to the Worthy Matron)

MARTHA:

>And Martha smiles through parting tears
>>At one whose heart and soul reveres
>The faith immortal that she knew
>>And placed within this pine for you.

(Martha presents her greenery to the Worthy Matron)

ELECTA:

> Electa's love is in this rose,
>> And may its symbol e'er repose
> Within two hearts whom God decreed
>> Should see our Star and know its need.

(Electa presents her flower to the Worthy Matron)

ASSOCIATE FLORAL MATRON *(holding satin bow)*:

> This satin bow combines and ties
>> The sentiments each flower implies;
> And you'll find doubled in its folds
>> The wishes of the blooms it holds.

(Assoc. Floral Matron attaches it to flowers, forming bouquet.)

FLORAL PATRON:

> No flower that's grown can quite express
>> The deep and lasting gratefulness
> Within the hearts of those you know
>> For all the attributes you show;
> Our thanks for serving us this year
>> Is tucked within this boutonniere.

(Floral Patron pins small flower on the lapel of Worthy Patron.)

Optional

(Matron and Patron are escorted to the position of Floral Marshal, who stands immediately west of the Altar.)

FLORAL MARSHAL *(presenting pen)*:

> Will you please take this pen in hand
>> And sign our Bible where you stand,
> That all who follow in your light
>> Will know what makes this page so bright.

(Matron and Patron sign the Bible, and are escorted back to the East.)

(The Floral Matron asks that the Chapter be raised for prayer.)

FLORAL CHAPLAIN *(at the Altar):*

Heavenly Father, in the sanctity of this room, where our souls find peace and our hearts find quiet, we behold Thy Written Word in deepest reverence. We ask a special blessing for those who place their names in close proximity to Thy Profound teachings; for there also have they placed their hearts and minds. As the disciples of Jesus sought to extend the knowledge of Thy Divine lessons, so have they, in their humble way, extolled the virtues of the Blessed Truth of Life. Amen.

(The Floral Staff retires)

4. Retiring Ceremony for Matron Who Will Become Chaplain
By Margaret Melissinos
(New York)

༯

The Floral Staff marches in to an evening hymn, and takes up positions on the floor.

FLORAL MATRON:

Worthy Matron, for 365 days you have held the reins of leadership in this Chapter, and have directed our righteous endeavors most admirably and effectively. But we are not here to bid you farewell—we ARE here to welcome you to your new office as Chaplain.

ADAH:

For three years, you prepared yourself for the office of Worthy Matron, but it takes four years of diligent application to duty to reach the venerated chair of Chaplain.

RUTH:

The office of Chaplain can only be administrated with humble dignity and quiet reverence. Your duties these past years have prepared you for the donning of this noble cloak.

ESTHER:

Although the office of Chaplain is an unassuming one, she is, in reality, our spiritual leader, and intermediary with God in all our supplications within the Chapter.

MARTHA:

The warm sincerity and humility that our Chaplain carries with her to our Altar will effect the demeanor and prayerful purpose of our communions with God.

ELECTA:

The Altar, which is a sacred and vital part of our Chapter proceedings, conveys spiritual comfort and inspiration to us, when our Chaplain kneels in prayer.

CONDUCTRESS:

Certainly, our Chaplain must be well aware of the fraternal responsibilities she carries, and mindful of her deportment in the discharging of her spiritual duties.

ASSOC. CONDUCTRESS:

Far from returning from the ranks, a Worthy Matron exalts herself in her cheerful acceptance of these holy duties, and her attentive concern for her devotional obligations.

EXTRA GIRL:

There is no glory nor homage accorded the Chaplain's position, except in the realm of Divine Recognition, which, most certainly, must accompany such a revered office.

ASSOC. FLORAL MATRON:

The office of Chaplain is a crowning climax to the long hours of labor and sacrifice that the office of Worthy Matron demands, and it is very fitting that her worthiness be recognized by the delegation of her services to this sacred trust.

(The Floral Matron requests that the Chapter be raised for prayer, as Floral Chaplain approaches the Altar.)

CHAPLAIN:

Heavenly Father, bless Thy servant, our Worthy Matron, for her devotion to righteous purpose, loyalty to Thy teachings, sincerity in all endeavors, and love for her sisters and brothers; all virtues designed in Thy Blessed Ways. Give her strength and guidance in the administration of her new office. Amen.

(Chaplain returns to her floor position)

SOLOIST *(appropriate hymn):*

FLORAL PATRON:

Worthy Matron, the seeds of love you have sown during your year as Matron have grown a beautiful garden of affection and admiration; truly a lovely setting for the beginning of your intimacy with God in our behalf.

FLORAL MATRON:

Worthy Matron, it is my sincere pleasure to present you with this bouquet with the love and affection of all your officers. Your entire Floral Staff wants you to know that this past year will make one of our happiest Eastern Star memories.

(At this point, each member of the Floral Staff approaches her respective Chapter officer, and personally escorts her from the room in retirement.)

5. Rose Ceremony Enrolling Retiring Matron into Past Matrons Group

A short ceremony which can be fitted to any number of Past Matrons present.

⤶

Past Matrons will form parallel lines between Altar and dais; each carries one red rose in her right hand. One P.M. will stand just in front of the Altar, facing the East, between the lines. As she finishes addressing the Retiring Matron, she walks between the lines to foot of dais, assisting the Retiring Matron down. Takes her left arm and always walks a little behind her, pausing before each P.M., who addresses the Retiring Matron and hands her a rose. Past Matrons face and each line alternates in speaking.

———

PRESIDENT:

Sister ————, in behalf of the Past Matrons of ———— Chapter, it becomes my great pleasure and honor to welcome you into our Past Matrons Group. May I conduct you through ———— Chapter's Rose Arbor? *(Goes to foot of dais.)* We will pause in our stroll down the path so that some of our Past Matrons may greet you.

(Stops in front of the first P.M. on south side)

2ND:

Sister ————, as you receive this rose, let it remind you that it bears with it the love and undying affection of all your Sisters and Brothers in this Chapter.

(Take a step or two and pause in front of first P.M. on north side.)

3RD:

This rose is a tribute of respect which your merit has won.

(Turn to next P.M. on south side, and so on until the end of the column.)

4TH:

This rose bears the recommendation and commendation of the members of the Chapter over which you have presided as Worthy Matron.

5TH:

I tender this rose as a token for the many unselfish hours you have given us during the past year.

6TH:

For your tact and diplomacy, I offer my rose.

7TH:

Because you had an ever ready ear for the call of want, or the need of sympathy, accept my rose.

8TH:

May this rose bring you a bit of that happiness which you have given to others.

9TH:

Because you truly exemplified that spirit of beneficence, fortitude, and steadfastness, I offer my rose.

PRESIDENT:

And, now that we have come to the end of our stroll, we

are happy to claim you as our Junior Past Matron and, as you lay aside the duties of the office, we individually, and collectively, say, "Well done, thou good and faithful servant."

(Retiring Matron is escorted to a seat and then other Past Matrons take seats.)

NOTE: Additional tributes can be given if there are more Past Matrons, or some may just hand Retiring Matron a rose.

6.   The Gol-Durn Rules of Past Matrons
By Ruth Adams, P.M.
(Arizona)

↩

Humorous Skit to initiate the Junior Past Matron into the Past Matrons Club.

Sister _____, before you can become a fully fledged member of our Past Matrons Group you must promise to abide by the rules of this organization. You will therefore repeat after me the following "Gol-Durn Rules" and promise faithfully to keep them sacred.

(These may be given by one person or split up and handed out to 10 Past Matrons.)

1. ALWAYS BE LATE for chapter meetings—that way you can get the attention to which you have become accustomed.

2. ALWAYS QUESTION in meetings the Worthy Matron's manner of handling the meeting. Discussions make matters so much more clear to the members.

3. ASCERTAIN FROM OTHER PAST MATRONS WHY various officers were appointed—this helps a great deal in promoting harmony.

4. ALWAYS BE READY to instruct the officers how to perform their work—they probably haven't been instructed by their Worthy Matron or Worthy Patron.

5. NEVER CEASE TO REMIND THE CHAPTER that 19__ was YOUR year and what happened of interest during that time.

6. NEVER LET AN OPPORTUNITY SLIP BY to express YOUR opinion regarding the way the money is being spent—it is usually TOO MUCH or TOO LITTLE.

7. NEVER HELP ON WORKING COMMITTEES—YOU are a PAST MATRON and as such are now entitled to rest on your laurels.

8. REMEMBER ALWAYS that you are not required to attend any meetings of the Chapter EXCEPT when Past Matrons and Past Patrons are honored—(you don't want to miss that free dinner and gift).

9. NEVER LET THE WORTHY MATRON FORGET that she is on 24-hour duty and keep a close check on her visits to the sick, shut-ins, visits to other Chapters, etc.

10. LAST BUT NOT LEAST—NEVER FORGET AND DON'T LET ANYONE ELSE FORGET what YOU did in your year—the officers YOU trained—the amount YOU gave for service—the way YOU handled certain problems—and on—and on—and on.

Sister _____, I give you a copy of the Gol-Durn Rules of the Past Matrons Club of _____ Chapter. Study them well, and if you put all these rules into practice and make a success of it—then YOU WILL BE THE BIGGEST "PEST" MATRON we have ever had.

TO HONOR THE WORTHY MATRON

7. *Bethlehem's Star*
An Installation Ceremony
By Cornelia Schatmeyer, P.M.
(New Jersey)

⤳

INSTALLING MATRON:

When the Star of Bethlehem appeared in the East almost 2000 years ago, we know God had placed it there centuries before and that He knew just how long it would take for its light to travel to earth and appear in the Heavens to announce the birth of the Infant Saviour in the Holy land.

Not too many years ago another child was born. God knew, even as before, that this new star would appear on *our* horizon in the form of Sister _____ who has been installed as our Worthy Matron.

MARSHAL:

Sister _____,

> *(Presents new Matron with floral centerpiece)*

There are many stars in the firmament
     And yours is not the least,
For although your star is a tiny one,
     It's as bright as the Star of the East.

May the light of your smile be always bright
　As you travel your road this year,
May each kindness you do come back to you
　In moments of gladness and cheer.

ADAH:

Without a star, the midnight sky
　Would really be too dark,
Without a Matron, our O. E. S.
　Would never make its mark.

You've proven your worth to all of us
　By efforts that never ceased
And, therefore, we were proud indeed
　To install you in our East.

(Places blue star in bouquet)

RUTH:

As stars, we are but little lights,
　But we will try to shine,
And thereby help to make this year
　One that is truly fine.

We promise to support each thought
　You have to serve our East,
And, as your duties are performed,
　May your happiness increase.

(Places yellow star)

ESTHER:

The stars cast but a tiny light
　On the velvet sky of night,
Helping travelers find their way
　As though in broad daylight.

You have traveled North, South, West
And stars above were bright,
They've led you to the honored place
In our Chapter room tonight.

(Places white star)

MARTHA:

Faith is shown by little things—
A star, a fern, a smile,
We pray it keeps you here with us
To serve us for awhile.

We know you'll find that greater strength
To help you on your way—
You've shown it by the happiness
You display from day to day.

(Places green star)

ELECTA:

You wish to live with your fellowmen
As though this day were the last;
This world will be a better place
As through it you have passed.

This is the plan that you follow
Every day you serve our Star;
May this ideal bring happiness
As you travel near and far.

(Places red star)

INSTALLING MATRON:
Let us offer prayer.

CHAPLAIN:

> We offer a prayer of thanks, oh God,
> That You have given us a Star
> Who understands our precepts
> And will carry them afar.
>
> Help her in her duties,
> Guard her on her way,
> And give her of Your store of love
> To serve us for many a day.
>
> Amen.

8. *Floral Ceremony for Installation*
By Margaret Melissinos
(New York)

⌣

Organist begins entrance march, "Evening Star," as lights are lowered.

Floral Staff march in, and fall into positions in front of the East, forming a cross, facing the East. At a given chord on the organ, the Floral Staff turn simultaneously and face the West. They proceed to their respective stations on the floor, near their officer counterparts.

———

FLORAL MATRON:

Worthy Matron, we are always deeply impressed by the solemn beauty and reverent import of our installation ceremony. However, I doubt if many of us pause to consider the seriousness of the vows which are written between the lines. With your kind permission, we will present our interpretation of what we believe to be the full content of your vows.

FLORAL MATRON *(turns and addresses the Floral Marshals):*

Sisters Marshals, will you please escort our Worthy Matron's proxy west of the Altar, and place her in a position of obligation?

(Floral Marshals escort the Associate Floral Matron to the Altar and she kneels.)

(The 1st girl approaches the Altar and stands near the proxy Matron.)

1st GIRL:

Do you promise that your eyes will see that which is not easily seen; that they will close when it would seem kinder that they do so, and that they will remain fixed on the true concepts which radiate from our symbolic Star?

PROXY MATRON:

Yes. *(She answers "yes" to each question.)*

(1st girl returns to floor position—2d girl approaches Altar)

2D GIRL:

Do you promise that your mind will remain open and eager for all knowledge in all respects; seek understanding in all things, and condemn no human frailties?

3D GIRL:

Do you promise that your footsteps will remain always in the path of Truth, and be constantly directed to the highest principles and ideals of our Order?

4TH GIRL:

Do you promise that your heart will beat in sympathy and compassion for your fellowmen, and that it will remain warm in the face of coldness; tolerant in the face of antagonism?

5TH GIRL:

Do you promise that your soul will remain in communion with God; exalted in that glory, and devoted to the teachings of Him, Whose Star we have seen in the East?

6TH GIRL:

Do you promise that your actions will always be governed by dignity and decorum, in complete accord with the propriety your high office demands?

7TH GIRL:

Do you promise that your ears will listen in fairness and discretion to all things that pass through them, and reject all that is petty, malicious, and unworthy of acceptance?

8TH GIRL:

Do you promise that your hands will move in fraternal beneficence, industry and devotion, and be ready always to extend comfort, warmth and assurance to a distressed sister or brother?

9TH GIRL:

Do you promise that your lips will move gently and cautiously, and never in haste, uncertainty or harshness; and that words unworthy of your high station will never pass through them?

(9th girl resumes floor position as Floral Patron approaches proxy Matron at Altar.)

FLORAL PATRON:

The vows you have just taken admit you to the highest office in this Chapter. Your perseverance in aspiring to this lofty position is proof of the type of person you are— and must be—to capably govern this body.

(Floral Patron resumes floor position as Floral Marshals escort Proxy back to her original floor position. Floral Chaplain approaches Altar, and Floral Matron asks the Worthy Matron to raise the Chapter for prayer.)

FLORAL CHAPLAIN *(kneels):*

Dear God, we pray for divine guidance for our Worthy Matron, her officers, and all those in attendance at this Chapter, that we may always follow the directives of Thy holy teachings which are inculcated in the beautiful rays of our Eastern Star. Bless always the activities of this Chapter, and keep them in accord with Thy blessed ways. We ask this in His Holy Name, Amen.

(Floral Chaplain returns to floor position)

SOLOIST: (Tune: *Remember*)

Remember this night,
 The night you vowed,
  "I promise," remember;
Remember the words
 You spoke aloud,
  "I promise," remember;
Remember the vows that keep you true;
Remember the faith we have in you,
Remember the Star that guides you, too,
And you will always remember.

(Floral Staff retires)

9. *One Light*
By Ruth Adams, P.M.
(Arizona)

⌣

To honor the Worthy Matron who has "Light" for her theme.
To be given on the first meeting night.

A.M.:

Worthy Matron, with your permission the officers would like to make a presentation.

W.M.:

You have my permission.

A.M.:

Sister ——————,

As Worthy Matron of ————— Chapter,
A privilege has been given to you,
To "tend the light" all this year
And lead us in ways that are true.

We know your light will shine
To bring others to its flame,
And tonight your light is so bright
We hope ours will be just the same.

All our lights shining together
Will brighten our Chapter's way,
And tonight we are happy to tell you
Our light we will ever display.

From Eccl. 11 chapter, 7th verse, we read: "Truly the LIGHT is sweet and a pleasant thing it is for the eyes to behold the sun."

A.M.:

Sister Conductress, please escort our Worthy Matron to visit her officers.

CONDUCTRESS:

Sister _____, Worthy Matron,
> Walk with me to seek the light
> Your officers will tend with you,
> For each one has a promise to give
> That they will be constant and true.

In Isaiah, the 50th chapter, 11th verse, we find these words: "Behold, all ye that kindle a fire, that compass yourselves about with sparks; walk in the LIGHT of your fire, and in the sparks that ye have kindled."

(They go to each officer in turn)

CHAPLAIN:

Sister _____,
> Here is one light for you to carry, *(gives decorated candle to W.M.)*
> One light for you to hold,
> One light to serve as a beacon
> As your helpers you now behold.

In Psalms, we may read: "For thou will LIGHT my candle *(lights candle)* The Lord, my God, will enlighten my darkness."

TREASURER:

Sister _____,
> I promise that my light will shine
> As bright as the coins I count,
> And I hope that the funds we gather
> All through this year will mount.

In Luke 12th chapter, 34-35 verses, we read: "For where your treasure is there will your heart be also. Let your loins be girded about and your LIGHTS burning."

ASSOCIATE CONDUCTRESS:

Sister _____,

    I promise that my light will shine
    As together we work for the right,
    And I hope that each new member
    Will be guided by our light.

In Psalms we may read in the 27th chapter, 1st verse: "The Lord is my LIGHT and my salvation. Whom shall I fear? The Lord is the strength of my life—of whom shall I be afraid?"

WARDER:

Sister _____,

    I promise that my light will shine
    So that peace and harmony will prevail,
    And the labors of our Chapter
    Will be a light that will not fail.

In John 12th chapter, verse 36, we may read: "While ye have LIGHT, believe in the LIGHT, that ye may be the children of LIGHT."

ORGANIST:

Sister _____,

    I promise that my light will shine
    In beautiful music each meeting night
    And, as we raise our voices in song,
    All members will feel our sweet delight.

In the 1st chapter of John, verses 4 & 5 we may read:

"In Him was life; and the life was the LIGHT of men; and the LIGHT shineth in the darkness and the darkness comprehended it not."

MARSHAL:

Sister ——————,

I promise that my light will shine
And I will walk in the Master's way,
For in His path our task will be light
As we work for others day after day.

In the 12th chapter of John, verse 35 we may read: "Yet a little while is the LIGHT with you. Walk while ye have the LIGHT, lest darkness come upon you, for he that walketh in darkness knoweth not whither he goeth."

SECRETARY:

Sister ——————,

I promise that my light will shine
As I record the good deeds of others,
And hope that all through the year
Our light will lead all Sisters and Brothers.

In Genesis 1st chapter, 3rd & 4th verses we may read: "And God said 'Let there be LIGHT,' and there was LIGHT. And God saw the LIGHT and that it was good."

ADAH:

Sister ——————,

I promise that my light will shine
And I will be faithful to each vow;
My emblem, the Open Bible,
Is the LIGHT to which we bow.

In Psalms 119, the 105th verse we may read: "Thy word is a lamp unto my feet and a LIGHT unto my path."

RUTH:

Sister _____,

I promise that my light will shine
And I will be constant in every duty;
My emblem—the gleaner's Sheaf,
Has a golden LIGHT of pure beauty.

In Matthew 5:16 we may read: "Let your LIGHT so shine before men, that they may see your good works, and glorify your Father which is in Heaven."

ESTHER:

Sister _____,

I promise that my light will shine
And I'll be loyal to kindred and friend;
My emblem—the Crown and Sceptre,
Represents light and joy that will never end.

In the 8th chapter of Luke, 16th verse, we may read: "No man when he hath lighted a candle covereth it with a vessel, but setteth it on a candlestick that they which enter in may see the LIGHT."

MARTHA:

Sister _____,

I promise that my light will shine
And my faith and hope will be strong;
My emblem—the broken column,
Represents the LIGHT of Him who did no wrong.

In John 12:46, we may read: "I am come a LIGHT unto the world, that whosoever believeth on me should not abide in darkness."

ELECTA:

Sister ———————,
   I promise that my light will shine
   In love and service day by day;
   My emblem—the cup of charity,
   Represents to us the LIGHT and the way.

In Psalms 43:3, we may read: "Oh, send out thy LIGHT and thy truth. Let them lead me; let them bring me unto thy holy hill and to thy tabernacles."

(Cond. escorts W.M. back to the East)

SOLOIST: *(appropriate solo)*

(After song, Cond. returns to station and A.M. and A.P. ask to approach the East. They have gifts for W.M. and W.P.)

A.M.

Sister ————————, Worthy Matron,
   We each have one light to carry
   As we walk the pathway with you,
   And we'll keep our light brightly burning
   To show that we love you true.

   It is with sincere pleasure
   That I present this gift tonight
   From your willing and working officers
   In this year as you "Tend the Light."

   We are glad to have the honoi
   Of working right by your side,
   And we know the year will be happy
   With you as our shining guide

(hands gift to her)

A.P.:

Brother _____, Worthy Patron,
We promise all our good wishes
Will reflect their light upon you,
For we are happy and proud indeed
To assist in all that you do.

For me—it is a special privilege
To present, on this special night,
A gift from _____ officers and
We know you believe in the right.

We are glad to be serving with you
And our light we will let shine,
Our hearts and our hands are willing
And this year will be just fine.

(A.M. & A.P. return to West after thank-yous)

TO HONOR STAR POINTS

10. *Precious Jewels*
By Ruth Adams, P.M.
(Arizona)

⤸

A Ceremony to Honor Star Points

W.M.

Sister Star Points,
   You form the beautiful central star,
   As our "jewels" you point the way
   By teaching the lessons of our Order
   And living them day after day.

   I am thankful that you are my "jewels"
   And I count each of you a treasure,
   For you help Our Chapter in countless ways
   And fill my life with much pleasure.

Sister Conductress, please present Sister Adah and all
Past Adahs for introduction back of Esther's station.

*(Cond. will introduce them and give the year they served.
Favors may be presented to each after verses. Present in turn
present and past Star Points.)*

SECRETARY *(stands a little in front of Adah's station):*
Sisters Adah,
  When the planner arranged our Star Points
  The first point was the heavenly blue,
  To symbolize Adah's virtues of honor and right
  And the vows to which she was true.

  As the jewel to represent her virtues,
  The lovely sapphire is a perfect stone,
  For it shines with integrity and truth
  Like you—Sisters Adah—our very own.

(hands out favors)

MARSHAL *(stands a little in front of Ruth's station):*
Sisters Ruth,
  The color chosen for the second Star Point
  Was golden yellow, like ripened grain,
  To symbolize Ruth's constant virtues
  Of humble obedience without thought of gain.

  The jewel of Ruth's true constancy
  Is the golden topaz of shining beauty,
  Which glows as a symbol of friendship
  As you—Sisters Ruth—follow your duty.

(hands out favors)

ASSOCIATE CONDUCTRESS *(stands back of Martha's station):*
Sisters Esther,
  The color chosen for the third Star Point
  Was white, representing light and joy
  To symbolize Esther's virtue of loyalty
  As her queenly right she did employ.

The jewel of her purity and courage
Is the diamond, sparkling and bright,
Which reflects all other colors
Just as you—Sisters Esther—reflect joy and light.

(hands out favors)

CHAPLAIN *(stands in front of Martha's station):*
Sisters Martha,
    The color chosen for the fourth Star Point
    Was Martha's own living green,
    To symbolize her faith and hope
    In things that are to us unseen.

    The jewel of Martha's faith and hope
    Is the emerald, so pure and so clear,
    Its beauty shines for all to see
    Just as you—Sisters Martha—walk without fear.

(hands out favors)

TREASURER *(stands little in front of Electa's station):*
Sisters Electa,
    The color chosen for the fifth Star Point
    Was the beautiful fervent red,
    To symbolize Electa's love for others
    As by way of the cross she was led.

    The jewel of Electa's love and truth
    Is the ruby which glows in a constant flame,
    Just as Electa's virtues of charity
    Are displayed by you who bear her name.

(hands out favors)

Soloist: tune: *May the Good Lord Bless and Keep You.*

> May the Good Lord bless and keep you
> Whether near or far away
> May our Star shine down upon you
> As you go your way
> May the veil of Jephthah's daughter
> Bring to mind fidelity;
> May the sheaf of Ruth remind you
> Of her constancy.
> May you always walk in sunshine
> With Esther's loyalty;
> May Martha's broken column
> Promise immortality.
> May your cup be overflowing
> With Electa's love and then,
> May the Good Lord bless and keep you
> Till we meet again.

w.m.:

> Sisters Star Points,
> > Sapphires, topaz and diamonds
> > Are precious jewels of great renown,
> > And emeralds and rubies, too,
> > Add beauty to every gown.
>
> > You Star Points are my "precious jewels"
> > And you represent the virtues you teach,
> > And though I have not riches or fame
> > I have you "jewels" within my reach.

(Suggested favors: Any small gift with their particular emblem stamped thereon; S.P. charm; S.P. pin, etc.)

1. Keeping Friends

Life is too short to be unkind,
Too short to be untrue,
For day by day, come what may,
There are many things to do.

Life is too short to waste the hours,
In bickerings and strife,
If passing hours bear lovely flowers,
We must give our best to life.

Life is too short to be little,
To harbor envy and hate.
The heart that is true enters through
Friendship's open gate.

A friend is something precious,
A jewel hard to find,
So keep your friend until the end,
And never be unkind.

11. Light of Thy Word
(Psalms 119:105-112; 19:14)
By Ruth Adams, P.M.
(Arizona)

〜

A ceremony to be used by Marshal preceding initiation. Place Star Point ribbons in a white bible which the Marshal will carry. Each Star Point rises when Marshal approaches and remains standing until Marshal bows after her final words.

———

MARSHAL *(speaks from her station):*

"Thy word is a lamp unto my feet, and a light unto my path.

I have sworn, and I will perform it, that I will keep thy righteous judgments.

I am afflicted very much; quicken me, O Lord, according to thy word."

> We are led by the word of God
> In ways of faith, truth and love,
> And as you teach His lessons tonight
> May you be guided by His Light from above.

(goes to Adah)

"Accept, I beseech thee, the free will offerings of my mouth, O Lord, and teach me thy judgments."

> The word of God teaches the story of Adah's courage.
> As she sacrificed her life for honor and right,
> She was prepared to fulfill her father's vow
> And thus her name remains as a shining light.

(gives blue ribbons)

(goes to Ruth)

"My soul is continually in my hand, yet do I not forget thy law
    Ruth's trust in the word of God
    Was constant and true all her days,
    She did not forget the law of His Light
    As she worked for others in humble ways.

(gives yellow ribbons)

(goes to Esther)

"The wicked have laid a snare for me, yet I erred not from thy precepts."
    Queen Esther faced snares and dangers
    But strayed not from God's pure light,
    Her bravery in asking favor of the King
    Saved her people from their desperate plight.

(gives white ribbons)

(goes to Martha)

"Thy testimonies have I taken as an heritage for ever; for they are the rejoicing of my heart."
    Jesus gave to Martha words of hope and light
    And her heart was filled with faith sublime,
    As her heart rejoiced in His kindness
    Her testimony became known for all of time.

(gives green ribbons)

(goes to Electa)

"I have inclined mine heart to perform thy statutes alway, even unto the end."

    Electa inclined her heart to acts of kindness
    To perform God's word to those in need,

She defended her faith in God to the end
And charity to others became her creed.

(Marshal goes to break in East line and speaks to all):

"Let the words of my mouth, and the meditations of my heart, be acceptable in thy sight, O Lord, my strength and my redeemer."

(Marshal bows to seat Star Points and returns to her station)

ADVANCE OR STEP-UP NIGHT

12. *Orchids in the Starlight*
By Ruth Adams, P.M.
(Arizona)

⟡

To honor Associate Matron and Associate Patron on Advance Night. With optional gift presentations. To be given just preceding ceremony of initiation. Have small basket for A.M. to carry—may have basket for A.P., too, if desired. If not, have blue orchid boutonniere for Adah to give A.P.

─────────

W.M.:

    Sister _____ and Brother _____,
        This is a happy night for us
        As we bring good wishes to each of you;
        Your hopes, and plans, and labors
        Have now made your dream come true.

        In your service to _____ Chapter
        You have been constant in every duty,
        And for all your past endeavors
        We want to fill this night with beauty.

        The familiar slogan, "Say it with flowers,"
        Is a way to say "We love you,"
        And because of your faithful service
        We also say—"Orchids to each of you."

Sisters Conductress and Associate Conductress, please escort the Associate Matron and Associate Patron to the East

CONDUCTRESS:

Sister _____,

> The starlight has been filled with dreams
> Ever since your initiation night,
> And now a dream is coming true
> As you walk in the rays of its light.

> Because of your years of service
> And love and devotion displayed,
> We now take you to orchids blooming
> To reflect the joy of this happy parade.

> It is with the greatest of pleasure
> I escort you on your Eastward way,
> To gather orchids that are blooming
> To add to your starlight bouquet.

(hands basket to her)

ASSOCIATE CONDUCTRESS:

Brother _____,

> You, too, have worked in the starlight
> To help our Chapter in many ways,
> We appreciate all your kindly deeds
> And are glad to bring you our praise.

> It is an honor and joy to escort you
> As you go to the East tonight,
> For we know your Masonic teachings
> Will shine forth in the Eastern Star Light.

(They are conducted to stand back of Esther's chair—leave

space so that Star Points may come to them with orchids. Each Point has an orchid of her color for basket and Adah has blue orchid for A.P., providing he does not carry a basket. Each turns and faces them from their own station and goes to them with the orchid after saying verse.)

ADAH:

> Sister _____ and Brother _____,
> > Blue orchids are sweetly blooming
> > In the starlight—just for you,
> > They speak of our fidelity
> > And of the vows to which we are true.
>
> > This "orchid to you" means to us
> > That you've been true in every way,
> > And we wish for you true happiness
> > As Adah's fidelity you display.

RUTH:

> Sister _____ and Brother _____,
> > Yellow orchids are brightly blooming
> > In the starlight—just for you,
> > They speak our promise of constancy
> > As we help you carry on through.
>
> > This "orchid to you" means to us.
> > That you've been constant day by day,
> > And we wish you pleasure in your service
> > To the teachings of each star ray.

ESTHER:

> Sister _____ and Brother _____,
> > White orchids are proudly blooming
> > In the starlight—just for you,
> > They speak our promise of loyalty
> > In all that you plan to do.

This "orchid to you" means to us
That you've been loyal, come what may,
And we wish for you joy and light
And hearts that are happy and gay.

MARTHA:

Sister _____ and Brother _____,
Green orchids are faithfully blooming
In the starlight—just for you,
They speak our promise of faith and hope
For a joyous future, bright and new.

This "orchid to you" means to us
That Martha's trust taught you to obey;
We wish for you a sincere faith
And God's blessing upon you we pray.

ELECTA:

Sister _____ and Brother _____,
Red orchids are vividly blooming
In the starlight—just for you,
They speak of our promise of love
And of our service for others, too.

This "orchid to you" means to us
That you've shown love in a kindly way,
We wish for you that love and friendship
Will be yours tonight in this bouquet.

W.P.:

Sister _____ and Brother _____,
As orchids bloom in the Starlight
Our good wishes are all for you,
We are proud of your achievements
And we think you are both "true-blue."

I'm happy to extend my welcome
And to say that now is the time
To take the steps as you advance
Along the Eastward climb.

SOLOIST: TUNE: "Orchids in the Moonlight"
When orchids bloom in the starlight
As tonight we honor you
You each will walk in the starlight
With success in all you do.
When orchids bloom in the starlight
They speak of Stars that advance
Though your knees be shaking
And your heart is quaking
As our "Stars" you will entrance.

Find your place in the Starlight
On this happy night
And the friends that you greet
Will be sure to repeat
Best wishes for delight.

There's a wish in the Starlight
As to the East you go
And the star beams that fall
Ever seem to recall
Love is all—love we show.

When orchids bloom in the starlight, *etc.*

Optional Gift Presentations

(Given before they return to the West)

CONDUCTRESS:

Sister ___________,

On this night of orchids blooming
You have really blossomed forth
Just as we knew you would really do
When you were chosen for the North.

The members of ________ Chapter
Are very pleased and proud of you,
For you exemplified each lecture
In a manner simple and true.

Because of your outstanding service
Again I say "orchids to you,"
As I present this gift from ________ Chapter
With best wishes for all you may do.

(hands gift to her)

ASSOCIATE CONDUCTRESS:

Brother ___________,

On this night of orchids blooming
You, too, blossomed out in perfection,
And, as you gave the lectures so clearly,
We were proud of our selection.

We know that you will fulfill each need
With care and precision next year,
And after this fine example of your work
We know we have nothing to fear.

So we also say "orchids to you"
For making this a night to long remember,
And with pleasure I now present this gift
With the acclaim of every _____ member.

(hands gift to him)

(Return to their seats after they have escorted the A.M. and A.P. back to the West.)

13. *Melody of Love*
(With Optional Gift Presentations)
By Ruth Adams, P.M.
(Arizona)

⤻

For Advance Night ceremony to be given immediately preceding ceremony of initiation. (Especially nice for A.M. who is named Jewel.)

W.M.:

Sister _____ and Brother _____,
   All through this year our theme has been
   The virtue of love that is blessed,
   And that love has truly been exemplified
   By you that have been seated in the West.

   Service and love you have freely given
   Whatever the need might be,
   And your fine spirit of cooperation
   Has been a joy and help to me.

   Because you have given love to others
   You now receive our love that is true,
   As we honor you this Advance Night
   With a Melody of Love just for you.

   Your Melody of Love has been happy
   As you've served your Chapter and friends,
   And we wish for you the time yet to come
   Will be a melody that never ends.

Sisters Conductress and Associate Conductress, please escort our Sister and Brother to the East by way of the Star Points.

(They proceed to the West; each has a small heart-shaped jewel case for the honorees to carry.)

CONDUCTRESS:

Sister _____, Associate Matron,
    Your Eastern Star Melody of Love
    Began on your initiation night,
    For when you saw His Star in the East
    You were inspired by its shining light.

    You've worked on many committees
    And served on each with a smile,
    You filled your office efficiently,
    Always ready to go that second mile.

    So we've a Melody of Love for you
    That we now wish to impart
    And, as you journey to the East tonight,
    You'll gather jewels of love in this heart.

(gives heart to her)

ASSOCIATE CONDUCTRESS:

Brother _____,
    Your Masonic Lodge in _____ *(city and state)*
    Taught you to serve your fellowman,
    And you have given your service to others,
    Always ready to help any way that you can.

    You, too, will hear our Melody of Love
    And this heart we give you tonight
    To hold the jewels of love you will gather
    As you go to the East and its light.

(gives heart to him)

(They are escorted to each star point)

ADAH:

Sister _____ and Brother _____,
   As Adah, I represent the daughter's love
   And fidelity shown for her father's vow;
   I give my jewel of love—Adah's symbol—
   The open bible, to which we bow.

(places miniature bible in each case)

RUTH:

Sister _____ and Brother _____,
   As Ruth, I represent the widow's love
   For husband and family in time of need;
   I give as my precious jewel of love
   A friendship bell which, with love, will lead.

(gives small bell to each)

ESTHER:

Sister _____ and Brother _____,
   As Esther, I represent a wife's pure love
   To country, God, and friend she was true;
   I give my own precious jewel of love—
   Our country's flag of red, white, and blue.

(places small flag in each case)

MARTHA:

Sister _____ and Brother _____,
   As Martha, I represent a sister's love
   For the family circle and for Jesus, too;
   I give this ring as my jewel of love—
   A symbol of perfection in all you may do.

(gives small ring to each)

ELECTA:

>Sister _____ and Brother _____,
>   As Electa, I represent a mother's love
>   Shown in service to others day by day;
>   I give as my precious jewel of love
>   The cross, the symbol by which we pray.

(places small cross in each case)

(They are escorted to stand back of Esther's chair)

W.P.:

>Sister _____ and Brother _____,
>   It is with deep and sincere pleasure
>   That I add my welcome tonight,
>   And I wish for you much joy and peace
>   May they be your guiding light.

>Our hearts are filled with a Melody
>Of Love that is joyous and true,
>As now _____ and _____, I say,
>Come to the East where we wait for you.

SOLOIST: TUNE: "Melody of Love"

>This is your Advance Night
>Filled with cheer
>Your work will be perfect do not fear
>While the Father guides you from above
>Here's our Melody of Love.

>Arm in arm together you will go
>You are shining jewels of love aglow
>Heaven sent you to us from above
>For our Melody of Love.

(After the song they are escorted to the East and the Conductresses return to their stations.)

〜 Optional Gift Presentations 〜

(Given before A.M. and A.P. return to West)

CONDUCTRESS:

Sister _____,

To have a part in our Melody of Love
Is truly a pleasure for me,
Because we have worked closely together
And in matters of service we agree.

Tonight we have been so proud of you
And your work so accurate and clear,
And we know the initiates were much impressed
As they walked in the light without fear.

Because of your friendship and service
Our Melody of Love is a happy song
And we hope will linger in your heart
With our gift to last all your life long.

(hands gift to her)

ASSOCIATE CONDUCTRESS:

Brother _____,

We are indeed proud of the excellence
Of your lectures of truth and of right,
For you exemplified the wisdom of working
For justice in God's own pure light.

So our Melody of Love has been for you
To tell you of our great pride,
And we'll be glad to help you any time
As we work next year side by side.

I now have the pleasure of presenting
A gift of love from your officer friends,
With the hope that the memory of this night
Will be a Melody of Love that never ends.

(presents gift)

(They are now escorted back to the West)

14. Daisies Do Tell
By Ruth Adams, P.M.
(Arizona)

⤸

Ceremony to honor Associate Matron and Associate Patron on Advance Night. Appropriate for A.M. named Marguerite or Daisy, or one who has chosen the daisy for her flower. To be given immediately preceding the ceremony of initiation.

W.M.:

Sister _____ and Brother _____,
   Tonight you advance up to the East
   And your hearts are beating fast,
   This is the night a dream will come true
   And we hope its memories will last.

   But don't be excited or worried
   And don't be the least afraid,
   For many friends are here with you
   So you really have it made.

   Before you start your visit to the East
   We have many good wishes to bring,
   These loving thoughts will cheer you
   And your hearts will start to sing.

Sisters Conductress and Associate Conductress, please escort our Associate Matron and Associate Patron to the East.

(Each has a small basket to present to A.M. and A.P. with few loose daisies to strew on the pathway before they start.)

CONDUCTRESS:

Sister _____,
>   You have worked faithfully for our Chapter,
>   Always ready and willing in time of need,
>   So when you were chosen for the North,
>   You gladly stepped out to take the lead.
>
>   There is a daisy flower called "Marguerite"
>   With petals of purest white,
>   And as you wend your way to the East
>   You'll gather daisies this joyful night.
>
>   You will also gather our good wishes
>   For tonight, and for the year that's ahead,
>   _____, we think you're a real "Daisy"
>   And we'll scatter flowers on the path you tread.

(scatters few daisy petals and hands basket to her)

ASSOCIATE CONDUCTRESS:

Brother _____,
>   You, too, have been a fine worker,
>   So friendly and so easy to please
>   And we know that in the East tonight
>   You'll be calm, and completely at ease.
>
>   We've good wishes for you by the score
>   To gather in this basket of reed,
>   And we hope that our good wishes
>   Will fill your every need.
>
>   Now is the time to make your "Advance"
>   As you go to the East to preside,

And it is an honor and joy for me tonight
To be your escort and your guide.

(scatters petals and hands basket to him)

(They are escorted to stand halfway between Esther's chair and the West. Star Points will address them. Adah and Electa advance to stand back of Ruth and Martha stations; they have daisies to give them.)

ADAH:

Sister _____ and Brother _____,
There is an oft heard saying
That "daisies never tell,"
But we don't have daisies like that
For ours are under a *(name of A.M.)* spell.

These marguerites are now telling you
We love you for your fidelity so true,
And that we'll be always faithful
And to you we will be "true Blue."

(gives daisies to each in baskets)

ELECTA:

Sister _____ and Brother _____,
My marguerites are now telling you
We love you for the love you've shown others;
We promise we will be helpful to you
And loving to our Sisters and Brothers.

(gives daisies)

(Adah and Electa return to seats together, while Ruth and Martha move to stand back of their chairs.)

RUTH:

Sister _____ and Brother _____,
   My marguerites are now telling you
   We love you for the constancy you've shown,
   And we'll be constant to our duties
   As you reap the good you have sown.

(hands daisies)

MARTHA:

Sister _____ and Brother _____,
   My marguerites are now telling you
   We love you for the trust you've shown;
   We promise we'll be loyal and faithful
   And that you'll never need to walk alone.

(hands daisies)

(They return to seats. Esther stands to side of chair and faces them.)

ESTHER:

Sister _____ and Brother _____,
   My marguerites are now telling you
   We love you for your joy and light,
   And we promise we will let our light shine
   Just as yours is shining tonight.

(hands daisies and is seated)

W.P.:

Sister _____ and Brother _____,
   As far as I'm concerned you're both "Daisies"
   And we think you are "Worthy," too,
   So it is a joy for me tonight
   To extend a warm welcome to both of you.

So come to the East as our honored guests
Who we welcome with much pride,
Everything is waiting here for you
To assume your stations side by side.

SOLOIST: TUNE: "Daisy, Daisy Give Me Your Answer True"

(A.M.'s name may be used instead of Daisy)

Daisy, Daisy, Daisy and ＿＿＿＿＿, too,
We're delighted—to have such a pair as you,
We won't have a single worry,
And you won't need to hurry
You'll both do fine—
Your light will shine
As you go to the East tonight.

(They are escorted to East after the song and the ceremony of initiation follows. Cond. and Assoc. return to stations.)

CHAPTER BIRTHDAY—CHARTER MEMBERS

15.   *Our Loving Hearts*
By Ruth Adams, P.M.
(Arizona)

❧

Program to honor any Chapter Birthday. Under Good of Order. Have birthday candles given to each member—not to be lighted until W.M. asks them to light candles. Have match packs cut in small sections and given to every other member.

W.M.:

Members of _____ Chapter,
A birthday is a happy time,
A time to count the years gone by,
A time to light our candles of love,
A time to laugh—but not to sigh.

We want our *(number of years)* birthday
To be a time of giving out light,
For 'tis more blessed to give than receive
And lighted candles make a lovely sight.

One little candle in a darkened room
Has a flame that is flickering and pale,
But a roomful of candles glowing together
Spread a light that will never fail.

(Star Points in turn say verse and place candle of their respective color on a birthday cake in front of East pedestal. Each lights her own candle. Each stands at her station to say verse, then goes to place candle on cake—lights it and returns to station.)

ADAH:

> Adah was born with a loving heart
> And to her father's vow was true,
> She gave her life for right and duty
> And wore a veil of heavenly blue.
>
> I represent Adah, the daughter's, station
> To tell of her fidelity to the right,
> And for all of _____ Chapter's daughters
> It's a joy to give Adah's blue light.

RUTH:

> Ruth, too, was blessed with a loving heart
> Always willing with others to share,
> She gave her labor each day for food
> And, as she worked, whispered a prayer.
>
> I represent Ruth, the widow's, station
> To tell of her devotion to duty,
> And for the widows of _____ Chapter
> I give Ruth's light of golden beauty.

ESTHER:

> Queen Esther, we know, had a loving heart
> Filled with loyalty for her people's need,
> She was willing to give her life for others
> And is famous for her courageous deed.
>
> I represent Esther, the station of the wife,
> To tell of her courage and might,

And for the wives of _____ Chapter
It is a joy to give her pure light.

MARTHA:

Martha was blessed with a loving heart
And gave her service of love each day,
Her belief in the Master's teachings
Led her always to walk in His way.

I represent Martha, the sister's, station
To tell of her faith in things not seen,
And for the sisters of _____ Chapter
It's a pleasure to give Martha's light of green.

ELECTA:

Electa, we know, had a loving heart
Filled with compassion for those in need,
She was willing to give her life for the cross
And loyalty to truth was her creed.

I represent Electa, the Mother's, station
To tell of her loyalty to truth and right,
And for the mothers of _____ Chapter
With truest love, I give Electa's light.

CHAPLAIN:

When the Master thought of gifts
He had these beautiful words to say,
"Tis better to give than to receive"—
This we should do—to live in His way.

We know you each has a loving heart
Always willing with others to share,
And at this time we'll gather your "light"
To make days for others more fair.

Loving is giving—giving is loving
It means the same whichever we say,
And for our *(Eastern Star Home or other project)*
Let us give in the Master's way.

(Have "candle-light" contributions gathered at this time)

W.M.:

A birthday is a time for singing,
A time for a birthday wish as you blow,
So please light your birthday candle
And think of a wish to make your heart glow.

After the singing is over—
And your birthday wish has been made,
Then blow out your little candle
With the light that will never fade.

(Have lights dimmed as they light candles. Suggested song: "The Angels are Lighting God's Little Candles." Immediately after song, W.M.*** and all sing "Happy Birthday"—then blow out candles. Have lights raised as candles are blown out.)

SUGGESTION: Have invitation to attend birthday party sent to every member and enclose a cloth candle to hold money pasted to it. Letter along the following lines:

Because we want our birthday to be a time of giving rather than receiving we give you this birthday candle with the hope you will "light" it through your contribution to the Eastern Star Home Fund (or whatever worthy project is desired), and bring it with you to our birthday party on the above date.

Our Worthy Grand Matron's (or W.M.'s) project this year is _____ and our goal is _____. We can achieve this goal with the help of your "lighted birthday candle."

Please come to our birthday party—the program will be worth your while—there will be time for fellowship—and you will have an opportunity to place your "lighted candle" on the birthday cake. If you cannot attend our party and want to "light a candle," you may mail your "light" to our Secretary _____.

Letter may be decorated with cake and candles.

16. Golden Years
By Ruth Adams, P.M.
(Arizona)

⤸

To honor those who have been members for 50 years or more. Note: This was given at Arizona Grand Chapter in 1960 at 11:30 A.M.—it is easier for the older members to attend during the day. May also be used by subordinate Chapter. A rose is given to each.

W.G.M.:

Sisters and Brothers—Our Golden Year Members,
   Golden are the years, and golden, too, the Stars
As we honor our Golden Year Members today,
   Each year of service is a golden star
   That sparkles with beauty in each lovely ray.

You Golden Stars are a shining example
   For through the years you have walked in the light,
You inspire us all to be faithful and true
   And strengthen our courage to work for the right.

So, it is with gratitude and with humility
   That I welcome you to (Grand) Chapter today,
For you are beloved and dear to us all
   And are truly living the Eastern Star Way.

W.G.P.:

Sisters and Brothers—Golden Year Members,
   I am glad to add my welcome to you

Our Golden Star Members so faithful and dear,
We admire you for your love for our Order
And for your loyalty and purpose clear.

You represent to us a true heritage
Of courage, faith, and all that is good,
For you've obeyed the vows of your obligation
And lived in peace and brotherhood.

NARRATOR *(from the East, Grand Secretary or a good
   speaker):*

The lessons of our beautiful Order
Have been learned and lived by you,
Your fidelity, constancy, loyalty, faith and love
Now shine as jewels of a brilliant hue.

When the planner arranged our Star Points,
The first point was the heavenly blue
To symbolize Adah's virtues of honor and right
And the vows to which she was true.

As the jewel to represent her virtues,
The lovely sapphire is a perfect stone
For it shines with integrity and truth
Like you—Golden Stars—our very own.

The color chosen for the second Star Point
Was golden yellow, like ripened grain,
To symbolize Ruth's constant virtues
Of humble obedience without thought of gain.

The jewel of Ruth's true constancy
Is the golden topaz of shining beauty,
Which glows as a symbol of friendship
As you—Golden Stars—follow your duty.

The color chosen for the third Star Point
Was white, representing light and joy
To symbolize Esther's virtue of loyalty
As her queenly right she did employ.

The jewel of her purity and courage
Is the diamond, sparkling and bright,
Which reflects all other colors
Just as you—Golden Stars—reflect joy and light.

The color chosen for the fourth Star Point
Was Martha's own living green
To symbolize her faith and her hope
In things that are to us unseen.

The jewel of Martha's faith and hope
Is the emerald—so pure and so clear,
Its beauty shines for all to see
Just as you—Golden Stars—walk without fear.

The color chosen for the fifth Star Point
Was the beautiful, fervent red
To symbolize Electa's love for others
As by way of the cross she was led.

The jewel of Electa's love and truth
Is the ruby which glows in a constant flame,
Just as Electa's virtues of charity
Have been displayed by you in our Saviour's name.

(Have all GOLDEN YEAR MEMBERS presented at this time, but have the 60 or more year members presented first.)

W.G.M.:

Dear 60 or more year members,
   A 60th anniversary is called the "Diamond"

And as 60-year members you are jewel bright,
Through years of service to our Order,
Like "Diamonds" you have reflected light.

So twinkle, twinkle Diamond Stars
As faithfully on your way you go,
We are proud of you and we love you
Because of the shining light that you show.

(50 or more year members are now presented and stand in line with 60-year members. Ushers and Pages escort and stand in line back of them.)

W.G.M.:

Dear 50 and more year members,
    Memories of more than fifty years
    Hold a wealth of dreams come true
    As hearts and hands of friends are joined
    In this meeting today with you.

May blessed peace dwell in your hearts
And may the blessings you've given others
Circle back again to each of you
Through the love of your Sisters and Brothers.

You have been strong and of good courage
And carried our Star within your heart
As a jewel of love to treasure
And from its teachings never to part.

So it is with sincere pleasure
That we give to each a rose—the symbol of love
And we now humbly add our blessing
To those from our Heavenly Father above.

(They are escorted to the East by the Grand Pages, who escort the men. Grand Ushers escort the ladies. The remaining Grand Pages form an aisle for them to walk through.

*As they are escorted to the East to receive their rose from
the W.G.M. a song is sung to the tune of "May the Good Lord
Bless and Keep You.")*

SOLOIST:

May the Good Lord bless and keep you
Whether near or far away.
May our Star shine down upon you
As you go your way.
May the veil of Jephthah's daughter
Bring to mind fidelity;
May the sheaf of Ruth remind you
Of her constancy.
May you always walk in sunshine
With Esther's loyalty;
May Martha's broken column
Promise immortality.
May your cup be overflowing
With Electa's love, and then,
May the Good Lord bless and keep you
Till we meet again.

17. *Spinning Dreams*
By Ruth Adams, P.M.
(Arizona)

Ceremony to honor Charter Members.

Have "Old Spinning Wheel" played during escorting. Gifts may be presented by Star points after they speak or all at one time by member designated. W.M. asks Cond. to present honored guests. After introduction W.M. speaks.

W.M.

Sisters and Brothers—our Charter Members,
With outstretched hands we welcome you
As we honor you here tonight,
For you're our very own pioneers
And you've led us in truth and right.

Our Chapter was formed in friendship
And friendship has filled the years,
With joy our cup has overflowed
Though now and then mixed with tears.

The dreams you spun in the long ago
Made our splendid Chapter come true,
And tonight to you—dreamers and builders—
Our thanks and love are extended to you.

W.P.

Sisters and Brothers—our Charter Members,
You were the ones who spun the dreams,

Yours were the minds that accomplished the plan,
Yours were the hearts with a purpose true,
And yours were the lips that said "We can."

(Cond. and Assoc. Cond. reseat guests at this time. Return to their seats.)

ASSOCIATE CONDUCTRESS:

Sisters and Brothers—our Charter Members,
Nothing is dearer than friendship
That grows sweeter as the years go by,
Nothing is sweeter than spinning dreams
Which come true—and which satisfy.

CONDUCTRESS:

Sisters and Brothers—our Charter Members,
Although you dreamed and planned a lot
Your hands were always busy too,
And without the labor of your hands
Your dreams never would have come true.

ADAH:

Sisters and Brothers—our Charter Members,
Like Adah, you fulfilled your vow
And built our Chapter hand-in-hand,
In friendship you worked together
And formed a true and faithful band.

RUTH:

Sisters and Brothers—our Charter Members,
Like Ruth, you were industrious,
Your hands were constant in their duty,
And though to others they appear worn
To us they are molded in beauty.

ESTHER:

Sisters and Brothers—our Charter Members,
Like Esther, you have proved to be loyal
When asked to take your stand,
Your wisdom and courage through the years
Have been to us a guiding hand.

MARTHA:

Sisters and Brothers—our Charter Members,
Like Martha, you were filled with hope
For a future strong and sure,
Your hands were joined together in faith
And your purpose was right and pure.

ELECTA:

Sisters and Brothers—our Charter Members,
Like Electa, you were generous and kind
And obeyed the Master's command
To always "Love One Another"
And, to those in need, lend a hand.

CHAPLAIN:

Sisters and Brothers—Charter Members,
There were many times in those early days
When you stopped in your busy way
To fold your hands and talk to God,
To fold your hands and to pray.

SOLOIST: TUNE: "Old Spinning Wheel"

There's an old-fashioned thing we call friendship
Spinning dreams of the friendship we love,
Spinning dreams of an old-fashioned Chapter,
And the maids of the long, long ago.

Sometimes it seems that we can hear these friendships
   calling
As the organ softly plays so sweet and low,
There's an old-fashioned thing we call friendship
Spinning dreams of a love that will ever flow.

W.M.:

Sisters and Brothers—our Charter Members,
   We're glad you dreamed in the long ago
   And glad you spun your dreams so well
   For without your dreams and your planning
   There would be no _____ Chapter story to tell.

TO HONOR PAST MATRONS AND PAST PATRONS

18. *Three-Ring Circus*
For Any Organization
By Ruth Adams, P.M. *(Arizona)*

⤴

Program to honor Past Matrons and Past Patrons.

With the invitations enclose a "comp" complimentary ticket bearing number of their year. Have affiliated P.Ms. and P.Ps. numbered the year they served preceded by an A. Decorations in circus theme. Program to be given under Good of the Order.

W.M.:

Past Matrons and Past Patrons,
  "How dear to my heart are the scenes of my childhood
  When fond recollection presents them to view,"
  Is a song that's familiar and dear to us all
  With its haunting refrain and its words all so true.

  We'll go back to childhood scenes tonight
  To that wonderful and happy circus day,
  And we'll remember all the funny things
  When we were children, light-hearted and gay.

  Past Matrons and Past Patrons of *(chapter)*
  You are to be our honored guests
  As we visit again the big three-ring
  And see the clowns with their tricks and jests.

W.P.:

Past Matrons and Past Patrons,
    Early in the morning before the sun was up
    The circus train came rolling into town,
    And everybody hurried to watch the cars unload
    To see the different animals and, now and then, a
      clown.

    There were gaily painted cages and wagons
    Which the elephants pushed with a will,
    And soon the lot was covered with tents
    In which the performers would show their skill.

A.M.:

Past Matrons and Past Patrons,
    Our guides will escort you to the tent
    Where you each will have a reserved seat,
    And then, once again, in fond recollection
    Your eyes will have a big treat.

    All the dear familiar circus things
    To your memory we will now recall,
    The sideshow freaks, the trained animals,
    And the clowns—both large and small.

A.P.:

Past Matrons and Past Patrons,
    The sideshows were held in smaller tents
    And the barkers had a long spiel,
    "Step right this way, Ladies and Gents
    See the man who eats fire for his meal.

    Come see the only living three-headed goat,
    See Miss Emma—the fattest lady in the land,
    Come see Mohammed, the giant, nine feet tall,
    And Carlos, the dwarf, who sleeps in his hand."

TREASURER:

Past Matrons and Past Patrons,
Oh! The sideshows were full of thrills for us
And the Bearded Lady filled us with wonder,
'Til we stopped to see the Sword Swallower
Who never once made a slip or a blunder.

But soon the sideshows were finished
And to the MAIN ENTRANCE we pushed our way,
So now get your tickets ready
For the Big Show—so lively and gay.

SECRETARY:

Past Matrons and Past Patrons,
You each have a complimentary ticket
To permit you to enter the Big Show free,
I'm sure you remember hearing of "comps"
And the shows you were entitled to see.

As the number on your "comp" is called
You will enter the circus ground,
There'll you'll find joys of your childhood
And your heart will begin to pound.

(Secretary reads names of P.Ms. and P.Ps. according to their year of service, filling in affiliates in their year. Cond. and Assoc. Cond. will escort them to the Big Show—have some sort of "entrance" fixed up to represent a tent, and as they enter the "tent" give each a balloon. Could give men canes or whips but balloons are cheaper and easier to find. After all have been seated in the "tent" (back to their seats) the program continues.)

CHAPLAIN:

Past Matrons and Past Patrons,
   As you went into the tent for the Big Show
   First you passed the animal cages,
   And there you saw lions and tigers
   Sometimes pacing back and forth in rages.

   There, too, you saw the tall giraffes
   Who can neither talk nor laugh,
   And there you saw camels and zebras
   All controlled by a man with a staff.

MARSHAL:

Past Matrons and Past Patrons,
   There were bears with shaggy heads
   From high mountains and from the north pole,
   There were seals that flapped their fins
   And caught a fish which they swallowed whole.

   There were leopards and jaguars, too,
   With stripes or spots on their backs,
   But best of all were the monkeys
   And their antics while begging for snacks.

WARDER:

Past Matrons and Past Patrons,
   There were lots and lots of elephants
   Trained to work or to walk in line,
   And the darling little ponies—
   How I wished that they were mine.

   Oh! It was such an exciting time
   And we gazed and we gaped in awe
   To see so many strange and hungry animals—
   They wanted their meat fresh and raw.

ADAH:

Past Matrons and Past Patrons,
    We reached our seats that were reserved
    Just in time for the Grand Parade,
    The sound of the trumpets—the roll of the drums—
    Will those memories ever fade?

    The band stepped out in bright array
    Playing the gayest tunes,
    We all were feeling carefree and happy
    With popcorn, peanuts and bright balloons.

RUTH:

Past Matrons and Past Patrons,
    The elephants trundled into view
    And they seemed like a whole parade,
    Wearing handsome blankets and headdresses
    And on their backs golden seats were laid.

    There were animals in painted cages
    Drawn by horses sleek and fine,
    There were acrobats, dwarfs and Indians
    And the cow-boys were to us divine.

ESTHER:

Past Matrons and Past Patrons,
    Yes, the Grand Parade was dazzling
    But the best was yet to be
    As we tried to watch all the big rings
    And decide which was the best of the three.

    The ringmaster blew his whistle
    And the band began to play,
    Plumed horses of black, and brown, and white
    Began to dance, and to bow and to sway.

MARTHA:

Past Matrons and Past Patrons,
 The trained dogs were in the middle ring
 Climbing stairs to slide down a chute,
 They jumped through hoops and turned flip-flops
 And Oh My! They were so cute!

 A trained bear rode a bicycle
 And another bear danced round and round,
 While the lions, too, had tricks to do
 With a trainer who was renowned.

ELECTA:

Past Matrons and Past Patrons,
 There were troupes of Japanese jugglers
 Who climbed up a high, high pole,
 And others who walked the tight wire
 With perfect balance and self-control.

 There was a man on the flying trapeze—
 How we marveled at his ease and daring,
 He swung back and forth way up in the air
 As with wondering eyes we kept staring.

(Cond. & Assoc. Cond. now have donned ruffs, clown hats, etc. and after they speak they pass out the gifts.)

ASSOCIATE CONDUCTRESS:

Past Matrons and Past Patrons,
 There were boomerang throwers in the center ring
 And the boomerangs obeyed their will,
 Next were the living statues in white
 Who amazed us all because they stood so still.

The trained elephants in one end ring
We really thought were the best of all
As they marched, and danced and frolicked around
And they even played with a ball.

CONDUCTRESS:

Past Matrons and Past Patrons,
There were clowns to keep things lively
In all sizes and in all shapes,
Some were on stilts, some were in cars
And some were dressed in women's capes.

They performed all sorts of funny stunts
And we laughed and laughed with glee,
For to see them imitate all the other acts
Was such a funny sight to see.

*(Pass out gifts—then after commotion has died down have
an appropriate song such as "I'm a Clown"—chorus should be
dressed as clowns. After the song the W.M. has the final
words.)*

W.M.:

We look to you Past Matrons and Past Patrons
With love and honor and pride,
For you each have had your own "Big Show"
As you stood in the East side by side.

It has been a joy for us tonight
To recall the scenes of long ago,
And we hope that our memories of the circus
Will make you think fondly of our "Big Show."

TO HONOR MASTER MASONS

19. King Solomon Had His Troubles, Too!
Master Masons' Night Program for Any Organization
Honoring the Masons
By Margaret Melissinos
(New York)

ᔪ

ASSOCIATE MATRON:

Worthy Matron, Worthy Patron, Distinguished Guests, Sisters and Brothers, on Master Masons' Night, it is most fitting to welcome our brothers in tribute and in pleasure. We hope that we have combined both successfully in our presentation.

ADAH:

We take you back in history
Three thousand years in span,
To one revered in Freemasonry—
King Solomon, the man.

RUTH:

He took an Apron and a Trowel,
A Compass and a Square,
And with a royal, firm avowal,
He raised a Temple fair.

ESTHER:

> He fashioned us a way of life,
> > Of love and brotherhood,
> That stretched beyond his country's strife—
> > A plumb-line road for good.

MARTHA:

> But then—within his palace walls,
> > His problems were immense;
> A thousand wives who roamed his halls—
> > Imagine the expense!

ELECTA:

> How could he ever keep in mind
> > Each anniversary day?
> If we would seek the truth, we'd find
> > That man had heck to pay!

CONDUCTRESS:

> His problems mounted by the score
> > With every brand new bride;
> How could he ever walk the floor
> > With every babe that cried?

ASSOC. COND.:

> He must have tightened many a veil
> > To quiet nagging tongues—
> But that would be to no avail
> > With healthy female lungs.

CHAPLAIN:

> Yes, Solomon must have had his share
> > Of trial and tribulation;

Just one wife needs a lot of care—
    He married a whole nation!

EXTRA GIRL:

He must have built that Temple for
    A little peace and quiet,
Where he could go and close the door
    Against that female riot.

ASSOC. MATRON:

A woman's always had her say—
    We know that to be true;
The only thing that's changed today—
    We share the Temple, too.

SOLOIST: TUNE: "Stranger In Paradise"

Welcome, all, to the Temple of Solomon,
We're happy you came to call—
    Good brothers of Solomon;
We'd like to share with you, in the Temple
    We all revere,
An evening devoted to your visiting here.
In song and rhyme we've been pretending,
Wending a path through time, in history,
When Masonry, in love unending,
And unity, raised a Temple sublime;
Here we are with our legacy, in our
    Temple of Solomon,
Reliving in memory, the wisdom of Solomon.
Again may we say we're glad
That you entered our open door,
To greet all the friends you had,
And make many more.

20. *Petticoat Lodge*
By Ruth Adams, P.M.
(Arizona)

ᕲ

Ceremony to honor Brothers—to be given under Good of the Order.

───────

W.M.:

> Brothers of _____ Chapter ____,
> It is with sincere pleasure
> That I welcome you here tonight,
> For as true Masonic brothers
> You are led by that Great White Light.
>
> We know you call us the "Petticoat Lodge,"
> But we know that you like us, too,
> For you're always ready to lend a hand
> Whenever there's hard work to do.
>
> We're proud to have you as members
> Of the Eastern Star in _____ Chapter,
> And we hope the joy of this evening
> Will ring out from every rafter.

A.M.:

> Brothers of _____ Chapter,
> On behalf of _____ Chapter,
> I, too, bring a welcome sincere,
> To your very own "Petticoat Lodge"
> Which we know you hold most dear.

We want you to have a badge to wear
As a symbol of this "lodge,"
The Conductress will now escort you
And don't anyone try to dodge.

(Conductress escorts Brothers to stand back of Esther's chair. Assoc. Cond. pins a "badge" on each one—a small white net petticoat. Each Star Point has bows of her color to pin on each one. If there are a large number of brothers have the Assoc. Cond. assist in escorting and have petticoats and bows pinned on by the flower girls.)

ADAH:

Brothers of Petticoat Lodge No. _____,

(add 1,000 to Chapter number)

We know you Masonic Brothers
To the Blue Lodge all belong,
And that color has much meaning for you
As you strive to do no wrong.

We also love the color of Blue
Which represents fidelity to right,
And I now give this bow of blue
To adorn your petticoat of white.

RUTH:

Brothers of Petticoat Lodge No. _____,
Yellow is the color of gold
And you have hearts of gold we know,
And so I pin on your petticoat badge
This tiny golden yellow bow.

ESTHER:

Brothers of Petticoat Lodge No. _____,
Your Masonic Apron and Gloves

Are of the purest white,
And I now give you a snowy-white bow
To speak of our great delight.

MARTHA:

Brothers of Petticoat Lodge No. ＿＿,
The evergreen is a symbol of yours
And to us represents a faith serene,
To adorn your snowy-white petticoat
I now add my bow of lovely green.

ELECTA:

Brothers of Petticoat Lodge No. ＿＿,
The red rose symbolizes love
And we share fraternal love with you,
To show our happiness tonight
I add my bow of red so true.

W.M.:

Brothers of Petticoat Lodge No. ＿＿,
Now your petticoats are beautiful
With the colors of our Star,
We hope you enjoy your new-fangled badge
And will keep it wherever you are.

We know a particular petticoat
Is your reason for being here,
And ask the Particular Petticoat of each Brother
To go and stand back of her dear.

We'll join in singing a song of love
Then each Sister will escort her Brother,
Back to his seat in the Chapter room
As they sweetly bow to each other.

We thank you for your work in our Chapter
And for being present tonight,
To be initiated into the Petticoat Lodge
And wear our badge of snowy-white.

(Sisters go to stand back of each Brother—all Sisters have slips of paper with words of song to tune "Together" which they sing to the Brothers.)

We've worked in Star together,
Laughed in our work together,
Sang love's refrain together,
And we know the Star sends its light afar.
One night we saw it together,
Walked in the Light together,
You're our Brothers dear
And we're glad you are here,
We always will be together.

(After song each Sister escorts her Brother back to his seat and bows to him and returns to her seat. Music of song during the escorting.)

PROGRAMS
TO HONOR GRAND OFFICERS,
STATE OFFICERS, DISTRICT OFFICERS,
HONORED MEMBERS

21. *Our Fair Lady*
By Ruth Adams, P.M.
(Arizona)

‿

Ceremony to honor W.G.M. or Deputy on official visit.

W.M.:

Sister _____,
On behalf of _____ Chapter No. _____
I welcome you on this special night,
We have anticipated your official visit
And made many plans for your delight.

To us you are as fair a lady
As any that can be found in books,
For you represent all the fair virtues
In spirit, as well as in looks.

You are "fair" which means gentle and kind,
You are "fair" which means honest and true,
You are "fair" meaning "light complexion,"
And "fair" meaning beautiful, too.

You well represent the "Fair Sex"
And in words and deeds are fair and just,
So as our Fair Lady of _____,
We greet you with sincere love and trust.

(W.M. requests Cond. to escort Honored Guest to visit the Chaplain and Star Points. Cond. has star for her to carry.)

CONDUCTRESS *(proceeds to East):*

Sister _____,
   There are many fair ladies in _____ *(insert state)*
   But you are the fairest this year,
   And it is an honor for me to escort you
   To visit other fair ladies that are here.

   This star you may carry with you
   To be adorned by the fair ladies you meet,
   Each will have a promise for you
   In a message that is loving and sweet.

(hands star to her)

CHAPLAIN:

Sister _____,
   The Open Bible is the center of our Star
   And its teachings lead us in His Way,
   May the light and truth of His Word
   Give you courage and strength for each day.

ADAH:

Sister _____,
   Fairest in all the land was Adah,
   Jephthah's Daughter, faithful and true,
   Who surrendered her life to fulfill a vow
   Wearing a veil of heaven's own blue.

Like Adah, you are fairest in the land
For you, too, are faithful and true,
And as a promise of our fidelity,
We give to you this Fair Lady in blue.

(places small doll dressed in blue on blue point)

RUTH:

Sister _____,

Among all the damsels in the fields
Ruth was the fairest, so we are told,
As she humbly gleaned for her daily needs
When the sheaves were yellow with gold.

Like Ruth, you are Fairest Among many,
Busy with your duties as they unfold,
And as a pledge of our constancy,
We give to you this Fair Lady in gold.

(places doll dressed in yellow on yellow point)

ESTHER:

Sister _____,

Thousands acclaimed Queen Esther's beauty
For she was filled with an inner light.
As she risked her crown, and life itself,
To save her people from their plight.

Like Esther, Thousands acclaim your beauty
And honor you for your adherence to right,
And tonight as our promise of loyalty
We give to you this Fair Lady in white.

(places doll dressed in white on white point)

MARTHA:

Sister —————,

    Altogether fair in word and deed,
    Martha placed her trust in things unseen
    As with assurance she raised her hands
    To ask comfort and help from the Nazarene.

    Like Martha, you are Altogether fair
    In word and deed you are calm and serene,
    And as our pledge of faith in you
    We give to you this Fair Lady in green.

    (places doll dressed in green on green point)

ELECTA:

Sister —————,

    Lovely and kind was the Elect Lady
    Who shared with others her cup and her bread,
    She lived in charity, truth and love
    And in persecution to the Cross she fled.

    Like Electa, you show Lovely kindness
    In helping others on the path you tread,
    And as a promise of our lasting love
    We give to you this Fair Lady in red.

    (places doll dressed in red on red point of star)

(Cond. and Honored Guest pause at station of Electa for song. Or may return to East if preferred.)

SOLOIST: TUNE: "Beautiful Dreamer"

    To you, Beautiful Lady, I raise my eyes
    My heart, Beautiful Lady, to your heart sighs

Smile, smile, Beautiful Lady, to one and all
As dear good friends fill our hall.
Smile, Smile, Beautiful Lady, and we'll smile too
With the rapture of friendship around us true,
Smile, smile, smile here tonight
Cares end, in the starlight
Love, Love, Beautiful Lady, we bring to you.

(A.M. requests permission to make presentation. Also, A.P. goes at same time if W.G.P. or Lecturer is present.)

A.M.:

Sister _____,

The virtues of our Fair Heroines
You show in your life each day
As you practice what you preach
By serving in the Master's way.

To you—our own Fair Lady—
I bring a gift of love and cheer
From the members of _____ Chapter
Who treasure your friendship this year.

A.P.:

Brother _____,

A beautiful lady needs a handsome man
To make a perfect pair,
And we are very fortunate
That together the Grand East you share.

"Handsome is as handsome does"
Is an old saying that's forever true,
And we think that you are "handsome"
In looks, as well as all you do.

We are glad to honor you tonight
Because of the friendship you give,
And hope this gift from _____ Chapter
Will be enjoyed as long as you live.

(A.M. and A.P. return to the West after thanks from guests)

22. *Dancing Belles*
By Ruth Adams, P.M.
(Arizona)

Ceremony for Honored Guest.

Need 1 tambourine and 5 dancing dolls—the kind that stand on a spindle and revolve like ballet dancers—dressed in Star Point colors.

W.M.:

Sister _____,

It is with much joy and happiness
We welcome you to _____ Chapter tonight,
As we bring you verses and songs of love
To tell you of our great delight.

We know you like a jolly good time
With every face smiling and gay,
And we know you also like to dance
When you take time out for play.

We thought we'd ask you to dance with us
So come join us with laughter and fun,
All work and no play makes Jill a dull girl
Don't ever be that kind of a one.

Sister Conductress, please escort our Honored Guest to the dance.

CONDUCTRESS:

Sister _____,
    We will trip the light fantastic
    And the music will gaily play,
    As I escort you around our dance hall
    To hear what our officers will say.

CHAPLAIN:

Sister _____,
    In biblical times the people were told
    To praise Him with timbrels and with dances,
    Tonight we rejoice in your visit to us
    With a "timbrel," songs of love and happy glances.

(hands tambourine to her when she says "With a timbrel")

(March tune is played as they go to the Marshal)

MARSHAL:

Sister _____,
    There is nothing better than a march
    To keep shoulders straight in line,
    And as our leader in all the grand marches,
    We know that you will do just fine.

(Waltz is played as they go to Adah—"Blue Danube")

ADAH:

Sister _____,
    A waltz that beats in three-quarter time
    Is a dance of beauty and grace,
    To whirl to the strains of the *Blue Danube*
    Brings happiness to every face.

    Adah ran to her father in joy at his return
    With timbrels in time to her dancing feet,

So, as a symbol of her faithful obedience,
I give this Dancing Belle, loving and sweet.

(places doll on tambourine)

("Yellow Rose of Texas" played as they go to Ruth)

RUTH:

Sister _____,

There's nothing so gay as a square dance
To the *Yellow Rose of Texas,* we all know,
But why is it called a "Square Dance"
When it is round and round that we go?

"Square" or "barn" dances are given at harvest time
Which Ruth celebrated in days of old,
So, as a token of her constancy to duty,
I give this Dancing Belle dressed in gold.

(places doll on tambourine)

("White Christmas" is played as they go to Esther)

ESTHER:

Sister _____,

To hear Bing's hit tune *White Christmas*
Fills our hearts with memories of home,
We want to dance 'round the Christmas Tree
And from family and friends never roam.

Esther was famous for loyalty to her people
As she pled for their lives in her royal gown,
And, as a token of her beauty and courage,
Is this Dancing Belle with a dazzling crown.

(places doll on tambourine)

("Wearin' of the Green" is played as they go to Martha)

MARTHA:

Sister _____,

An Irish jig expresses joy and hope
When *Wearin' the Green* is the tune,
For it has a happy, lively rhythm
To dance to any time of the moon.

Now Martha walked in quiet ways
And a *jig* she would *never* dance,
But as a reminder of her living green
This Dancing Belle I'm sure will entrance.

(places doll on tambourine)

("Lady in Red" played as they go to Electa)

ELECTA:

Sister _____,

The tango is a dance of romance and love
When the tune is *The Lady in Red*
The charm and beauty of this Latin dance
Will go right straight to your head.

Oh, the Lady in Red was truly beautiful
And our own "Electa Lady" was beautiful, too,
So, as a token of her love for others,
Is this Dancing Belle-just for you.

(places doll on tambourine)

(Song "Three O'clock in the Morning" as she stands in front of Electa. She is then escorted back to the East—or, if preferred, song may be after she has returned to the East.)

W.M.:

Sister _____,
You've danced your way into our hearts

For you're an example of the good and the true,
And the friendship and good will you scatter
Will reflect its light back to you.

And as the years pass swiftly by
We wish happiness and content for you,
And hope your heart will keep right on dancing
Though your feet may forget what to do.

(A.M.—and A.P. if W.G.P. is present—approach East with gifts)

A.M.:

Sister _____,

Although our dance of joy is over
We hope it will live in your heart,
And that our little Dancing Belles
Will always fill an important part.

The tunes that we played were only a part
Of the many good wishes we bring you,
For we know the virtue of each Dancing Belle
Is found deep in your heart so true.

As a token of our friendship and love
I present this gift from _____ Chapter,
Which we hope will always remind you
Of this dancing night of fun and laughter.

A.P.:

Brother _____,

We are honored and happy to greet you
On this official visit dancing night,
For we know you, too, like a jolly good time
With Stars twinkling bright in the light.

You've been called by many names this year
_____, _____, _____ and _____ too,
(insert names which apply)
So we didn't know just what to call you
That would be different and yet be true.

Finally, after thinking of many good names
And searching the dictionary through to the end,
As we present this gift with friendship and love
We found no better name to call you than—Friend.

(A.M. & A.P. return to West after thanks from guests)

23. *Do-Re-Mi Musical*
By Ruth Adams, P.M.
(Arizona)

◡

Ceremony for Honored Guests

Needed: small basket for Cond. give Guest and notes of her colors for each officer to place in basket—after saying verse. Appropriate for one who sings or plays musical instrument.

———————

W.M.:

Sister —————————,

    Tonight we have planned a musical
    To entertain you in a fashionable way
    And although we are not all singers
    We hope you'll understand what we say.

    We'll say it with music—beautiful music
    Over and over—we are glad you are here,
    For you're our very own Prima Donna
    With a voice to charm every ear.

    Many of us can't carry a tune
    We just hum—or speak in one key,
    But we're here to do our very best
    To greet you from G to high C.

W.P.:

Sister —————————,

    If I could sing in any style
    Right now I would burst into song,

But words of praise are mine instead
As I say we're glad you came along.

As our very own Prima Donna
You have a special place in our hearts,
And each tenor, baritone, soprano and alto
Want to join in with their parts.

(W.M. asks Conductress to escort Honored Guest around the music hall.)

CONDUCTRESS:

Sister _____,
    Unless it is in a basket
    I simply can't carry a tune,
    So I've brought a basket for you to carry
    To gather notes from those who can croon.

(hands basket to her)

(They go to officers in turn—each officer places a musical note in basket after saying verse.)

TREASURER:

Sister _____,
    Do-re-mi are notes of the scale
    And also—do-re-mi means money,
    We hope you'll have lots of do-re-mi
    To keep your life bright and sunny.

CHAPLAIN:

Sister _____,
    Thy word is a lamp unto my feet
    A light to my path each night,

(or use her own scripture)

Will be a Psalm that will lead you
On the pathway of Eastern Star light.

ASSOCIATE CONDUCTRESS:

Sister _____,
    Fa-so-la are more notes of the scale
    To run and to trill with delight,
    And we hope that all this year
    Runs and trills will keep your life bright.

MUSICIAN:

Sister _____,
    Ti-do are the last two notes of the scale,
    As musicians, we share harmony together,
    You are writing a score of music this year
    That will be gay and light as a feather.

WARDER:

Sister _____,
    As you run the scale of musical notes,
    We hope no discord will be found
    For we wish that peace and harmony
    May everywhere abound.

MARSHAL:

Sister _____,
    As conductor of our orchestra this year
    A baton will be something you'll need,
    You may keep the tempo just as you please—
    Slow-moderate-fast-faster-or fastest speed.

SECRETARY:

Sister _____,

   As you write the score of *(insert proper year)*
   You'll have notes of flats and sharps
   And we truly hope each bar will be
   Filled with rhythm of trumpets and harps.

ADAH:

Sister _____,

   We Star Points form a little choir
   To sing a carol of faith, truth and love,
   And through this year of _____
   May you be guided by His Light from above.

RUTH:

Sister _____,

   I join in the carol of love and faith
   With a wish for constancy's rich tone,
   We promise devotion all through the year
   And that you will never walk alone.

ESTHER:

Sister _____,

   I join in the carol of faith and love
   To add a strain of courage and light,
   For these qualities are always needed
   To make the music sound just right.

MARTHA:

Sister _____,

   I join in the carol of faith and truth
   To add mystery and beauty of hope,
   For hope adds depth and perception
   To the happiness for which we grope.

ELECTA:

Sister _____,

I join in the carol of truth and love
To add notes of kindness and zeal.
For kindness adds sweetness to every song
As we express the joy that we feel.

(Guest is escorted back to the East)

SONG: "Do-Re-Mi" *(words are real cute and do not need
to be changed to fit in with program.)*

W.M.:

Sister _____,

We tried to plan our musical evening
To include familiar words for your delight,
And also include favorite thoughts of mine
In a combination of music and light.

May the Light of God's love surround you
With music of heavenly peace,
And may His words be a comfort and blessing
That all through the year will not cease.

*(A.M. and A.P. proceed to East with gifts for Honored
Guests.)*

A.MATRON:

Sister _____,

Sharps and flats, notes, bars and clefs
Form a score you can easily read,
And we know that as you follow the score
You will be bound to succeed.

Music is inspired by the Light of His Word
To be in tune with all Sisters and Brothers,
And we know your year of Eastern Star work
Will be to the benefit of many others.

As the finale of our musical evening,
It is an honor and privilege for me
To present this gift from _____ Chapter
With our song of love in every key.

(presents gift)

A.PATRON:

Brother _____,
I'm not a singer or a crooner
And I don't play a horn or a guitar,
But I am here as a representative
Of _____ Chapter, Order of the Eastern Star.

We feel that your Masonic teachings
Led you to the truth of His Word,
And thus you worked in faith and love
So great honors on you were conferred.

We're glad to have you visit us
On this night of music and light,
And on behalf of _____ Chapter,
I present this gift for your delight.

(presents gift)

(A.M. and A.P. return to West after thank-yous)

24. *Night of Smiles*
By Ruth Adams, P.M.
(Arizona)

⌒

Ceremony for Honored Guest who has Smiles as a theme.

Guest will remain standing in the East for Ceremony until she is to be escorted to Chaplain and Marshal for presentation of Service gifts. This helps make it smoother when Chapter room is small.

honor Secretary _____

W.M.:

Sister _____,
   Friendship is a precious gift
   We give to those we love,
   A warm handclasp and a friendly smile
   Is inspired by the One above.

   Tonight we have a great big smile
   For you, *our* _____ *Secretary* Dear,
   And we hope you'll give it back to us
   And smile from ear to ear.

   A smile is just the badge to wear,
   It is always in good style
   So welcome to _____ Chapter
   As we smile—and smile—and smile.

give vase

W.P.:

Sister _____,
> I, too, have a warm welcome for you
> Because of the Service we share,
> I'm glad you're here with us tonight
> And I like the smile that you wear.
>
> For a smile can bring the sunshine
> To a day that is dull and gray,
> You bring to us a silver lining
> And I hope you'll enjoy your stay.

SECRETARY *(has large letter "S"):*

Sister _____,
> "S" to us stands for Secretary,
> The office of records to keep,
> And "S" also stands for a smile
> That will brighten each day as we reap.

> *(goes with letter to stand by Adah)*

ADAH:

Sister _____,
> Welcome to our "Night of Smiles,"
> We hope your worries will be few;
> As tribute to your fidelity,
> I add my flowers of Adah's blue.

(attaches spray of blue flowers to letter. Adah holds the "S" letter & flowers.)

CONDUCTRESS *(has letter "M"):*

Sister _____,
> "M" stands for the Merry Moments
> You have added with your gay smile,

And "M" also stands for ＿＿＿＿ Grand **MATRON**
Who is of a sweet and charming style.

(goes to stand by Ruth)

RUTH:

Sister ＿＿＿＿＿,
Welcome to our "Night of Smiles,"
When we all wear a smile just for you,
As tribute to your constant devotion,
I add Ruth's flowers of yellow hue.

(places spray of yellow flowers at base of letter. Ruth takes it to hold.)

A.M. *(has letter "I"):*

Sister ＿＿＿＿＿,
"I" stands for the instructions you give
In the lessons of Eastern Star,
It also stands for the intelligence
Which will carry you afar.

(goes to stand near Esther)

ESTHER:

Sister ＿＿＿＿＿,
Welcome to our "Night of Smiles,"
We hope that joy is yours tonight;
As as tribute to your loyalty,
I add Esther's flowers of purest white.

(adds spray of white flowers at base of letter—Esther holds letter.)

ASSOCIATE CONDUCTRESS *(has letter "L"):*

Sister _____,
"L"—of course—stands for Love
Which, when given to others, returns two-fold,
"L" also stands for the everlasting Light
The members of our Star behold.

(stands near Martha)

MARTHA:

Sister _____,
Welcome to our "Night of Smiles,"
We hope your smile will stay serene,
As tribute to your faith and hope
I add my fern of Martha's green.

(places fern at base of letter—holds letter)

TREASURER *(has letter "E"):*

Sister _____,
"E" stands for Enthusiasm for Eastern Star
That leads us all by His Light,
It also stands for the Eternal truth
And our seeking for the right.

(stands by Electa)

ELECTA:

Sister _____,
Welcome to our "Night of Smiles"
As our sincere love we now disclose,
As tribute to your love for others,
I add my flower—Electa's red rose.

(places spray of roses at base of letter "E." Electa holds letter. Star points go to West and place letters in a rack on a

large shield or badge to form the word "SMILE"; then return to seats.)

W.M.:

Sister _____,

Now you see our Chapter room
Wears a smile from ear to ear,
And the reason for our great big smile
Is just because you are here. our Secretary dear.

We hope you'll come back often
And be our honored guest,
For you have a motto we love to share
"A Smile"—and I think it's the best.

SONG: "The Sunshine of Your Smile."

(W.M. requests Cond. to escort Guest to gather gifts of service. They go to Chaplain and Marshal.)

CHAPLAIN:

Sister _____,

In the Holy Bible you found these words
"Serve the Lord with Gladness"

(or her own scripture may be used)

And all this year we'll wear a smile
That will banish any sadness.

To serve the Lord with gladness
We have our offering of service to bring,
To add to your worthy project
And help make a heart to sing.

(hands her envelope containing gift for Service project)

MARSHAL:

Sister _____,

    Our Eastern Star Home Maintainance Fund
    Is a project dear to your heart,
    And as we serve the Lord with Gladness
    For the Home we too will do our part.

    We have a contribution from our Chapter
    For the Home Maintainance Fund you hold dear,
    And as we served in this project of love
    It has been a joy to work all this year.

(presents gift for OES HOME FUND)

(They return to East to the music of "Sunshine of Your Smile" or "Smiles.")

A.M. *(goes to East to present personal gift from Chapter):*

Sister _____,

    You've a smile that makes us happy
    You've a smile that makes us gay,
    You've a smile that starts us smiling
    As we go our daily way.

    We're glad you share with our Chapter
    In choosing a SMILE to wear,
    For a smile adorns our face
    Just like flowers adorn our hair.

    It is an honor and privilege for me
    To present this gift from _____ Chapter,
    And we hope it will bring a smile
    That will stay in your heart foreverafter.

(hands gift to her)

(A.M. returns to West and A.P. proceeds to East with gift for W.G.P. or Lecturer, if present.)

A.P.:

Brother _____,
> You also wear a smile that's wide
> And comes straight from your heart,
> We're glad you closed the store tonight
> To be here for this particular part.

> Smiling *(first name)* the _____ store man
> Is what you are known to be,
> And you wait upon your customers
> With a smile just as nice as can be.

> We know you'll soon be hurrying home
> To keep things going right in the store,
> And we hope this gift from _____ Chapter
> Will be a treasure that you will adore.

(hands gift to him)

Song: *to the tune of* "Sam the Old Accordian Man"

(W.P. returns to West)

NOTE: *If preferred, the letters may be standing on the Secy. and Treas. desks and pedestals of Cond., A.M. and Assoc. Cond. and left there for the evening. After each Star Point speaks she would go and place flowers on letter and return to seat—in that way the "smile" would go around the room.*

25. Harvest of Joy
By Ruth Adams, P.M.
(Arizona)

↰

For Honored Guest whose theme is SHARING, *or whose emblem is the* SHEAF. *Suitable for* GRAND ADAH. *To be used in the fall.*

———————

W.M.:

Sister ——————,
    It is with JOY and happiness
    That I welcome you tonight,
    For at this harvest season
    The world seems gay and bright.

    We all are thankful for many things
    As we count our blessings each day,
    And ———— Chapter is especially glad
    As you visit us in your friendly way.

    With pleasant words and kindly deeds
    You have shared with Sisters and Brothers,
    And in appreciation of all your love
    We, too, want to share with others.

W.P.:

Sister ——————,
    I am happy to add my welcome
    At this harvest time of reaping,
    And tell you that the love you've shown
    Will come back into your keeping.

By bearing the burdens of others
And doing good day after day,
You have been a worthy example
Of living the Eastern Star way.

(W.M. requests the Cond. to escort Honored Guest to gather a Harvest of Joy. Cond. has basket cornucopia painted gold with some fruit already in it.)

CONDUCTRESS:

Sister _____,

You chose as your emblem the Sheaf of Ruth
Which, as an emblem of plenty, is known,
And in this year of sharing for others
Good deeds and good thoughts you have sown.

This cornucopia is called a "horn of plenty"
To be filled with a harvest for you,
As now we will visit each point of the Star
And you may gather flowers of every hue.

CHAPLAIN:

Sister _____,

Before you start on your way I want to remind our
members of the scripture which has been your guide:
_____*(insert her scripture here)*.
May each of us keep this scripture before us and try
to live by its teachings each day. In so doing our
lives will be useful and happy and will radiate JOY
into the lives of others.

(They continue on to the Star Points—each has a flower of her color with money wrapped around the stem, which they place in the "horn of plenty" after saying verse.)

ADAH:

Sister _____,

   To help fill your horn of plenty
   The blue of Adah's own sweet flower
   Represents your fidelity to honor and right
   As you've been led by the hand of His power.

RUTH:

Sister _____,

   The yellow flower of the humble gleaner
   Speaks to us of constancy to duty,
   And I have gathered Ruth's golden flower
   For in many ways you reflect her beauty.

ESTHER:

Sister _____,

   I have gathered a lily—pure and fair—
   To add to your horn of gold
   For you've shown courage and loyalty
   Just as Queen Esther in the days of old.

MARTHA:

Sister _____,

   I have gathered the lovely green fern
   That a living harvest you may reap,
   You've shown that Martha's faith and hope
   Bring inspiration to always keep.

ELECTA:

Sister _____,

   A red rose I gathered for your harvest,
   A rose of love and service for others,
   Like Electa, you have served a cause
   By helping needy Sisters and Brothers.

(Cond. escorts her back to the East, and returns to her station)

SONG: Suggest *Bringing in the Sheaves* or *Harvest Moon,*
    or any appropriate song.

W.M.:

Sister _____,

In your golden horn of plenty
You have fruit and flowers of autumn hue,
And it's a JOY to have the privilege
Of sharing our harvest with you.

Your service has not been for self—
'Tis for Jesus—for Others—Yourself last,
And we know that by sharing our blessings
The future will bloom like the past.

(A.M. goes to East for presentation of gift)

A.M.:

Sister _____,

It is indeed a JOY for me
To present a gift to you tonight,
And to tell you that you represent
The teachings of JOY and light.

We know that you are sharing
All your thoughts and strength each day,
To make this year of Grand Service
Useful and perfect in every way.

We are happy to honor you tonight
And tell you we're glad you are here,
We hope this gift from _____ Chapter
Will be treasured for many a year.

(Music of her song played as A.M. returns to the West)

26.   Our Silver Belle
By Ruth Adams, P.M.
(Arizona)

‿

Ceremony for Honored Guest at Christmas season visit. Especially appropriate for one who has white or silver hair, or whose name is Belle.

―――――――――

W.M.:

Sister _____,

> I'm happy to welcome you to our Chapter
> Especially at this time of the year,
> For Christmas is a joyous time
> As we greet friends that we hold dear.
>
> You are a very dear friend of ours
> And have been from the very start,
> So, tonight we all want to tell you
> How we feel in every heart.

(She requests Cond. to escort Guest to each officer. Cond. has a small Christmas tree and each officer will have a silver bell to hang on it.)

CONDUCTRESS:

Sister _____,

> Christmas just wouldn't be Christmas
> Without a Christmas tree to trim,
> And we have one for you to carry
> As we will decorate each limb.

(hands tree to her)

W.M.:

Sister _____,

    I'm glad to be the first of all
    To hang a bell upon your tree,
    And wish that your heart may be filled
    With Christmas joy and Christmas glee.

    There's much we want to thank you for
    Dear _____, our own Silver Belle,
    And as we trim your little tree
    Good wishes to you we will tell.

Treasurer:

Sister _____,

    My silver bell rings in friendship
    As we remember many happy days,
    We appreciate all your kindness
    As you taught us in Eastern Star ways.

Chaplain:

Sister _____,

    In the Holy Bible we read St. Luke's story
    Of Jesus, our dear Saviour's birth,
    And we learn of the angel's singing
    Joy to the world and peace on earth.

    There we may read of the lowly stable
    Where the light shone all around,
    And the Three Wisemen knelt in worship
    And the bells made a lovely sound.

Associate Conductress:

Sister _____,

    Silver bells—silver bells are ringing

As they play our *(name)* 's tune,
Which we know is *(insert motto)*
In the light of the silver moon.

A. PATRON:

Sister _____,
  Silver bells are sweetly ringing
  As we tell you of our love,
  My silver bell brings a wish for you
  To be guided each day from above.

A. MATRON:

Sister _____,
  Silver bells—silver bells are ringing
  In every member's heart tonight,
  And the silver bell I bring to you
  Holds a wish for joy and light.

WARDER:

Sister _____,
  My silver bell rings out to you
  Of the peace and harmony you teach,
  And with it comes our sincere wish
  For happiness and love within reach.

SENTINEL *(this may be omitted unless one has taken his place before ceremony)*:

Sister _____,
  Hear the silver bells of friendship
  As of happiness they sing tonight,
  And of the joy you bring to us
  As together we work toward the light.

ORGANIST:

Sister ⸺,
    Silver bells are softly ringing
    Ting-a-ling, a-ling, a-ling,
    We hope that when you hear them
    Your heart will gaily sing.

MARSHAL:

Sister ⸺,
    Silver bells in each small corner
    Ring out a song of love for you
    And tell you of our sincere thanks
    For all the work you help us do.

SECRETARY:

Sister ⸺,
    The bells are ringing merrily
    As in friendship we gather to tell
    That over, and over, and over again
    We have fallen under your spell.

W. PATRON:

Sister ⸺,
    Though silver bells may seem repetitious,
    Mine is ringing so that everyone knows
    I, too, have a welcome and wish for you
    Happiness and joy that grows and grows.

ADAH:

Sister ⸺,
    We're proud to call you "Our Silver Belle"
    For you live in honor and right,
    And the silver bells of friendship
    Sparkle brightly here tonight.

RUTH:

Sister _____,
We're glad that you're our Silver Belle
For you are faithful to every duty,
And the silver bells of friendship
Twinkle in shining beauty.

ESTHER:

Sister _____,
We're happy you're our Silver Belle
Because of courage and loyalty you show,
And the silver bells of friendship
Send out a constant warming glow.

MARTHA:

Sister _____,
We're pleased that you're our Silver Belle
For your faith is strong and pure,
And these silver bells of friendship
Will ever and ever endure.

ELECTA:

Sister _____,
We're delighted you're our Silver Belle
For your love for others you've shown,
And these silver bells of friendship
Are the sweetest we've ever known.

SONG: TUNE: "Christmas Time" (*known more commonly as* "Silver Bells")

(*insert Chapter name in blanks*)
_____ Chapter _____ Chapter
Dressed in holiday style

In the air there's a feeling of Christmas
Members laughing, members passing—giving smile
    after smile
And in every small corner you'll hear
Silver bells—Silver bells
It's Christmas Time in _____
Here the silver bells go ring-a-ling
Silver bells—hear them ring
Silver Bells—soon it will be Christmas Day.

    _____ Chapter _____ Chapter
See the star light
Shining forth its bright rays
As the members assemble for their meeting
Hear the singing—see the friends smile
This is _____'s big night
And above all this hustle you hear
Silver bells—Silver bells, *etc.*

W.M.:

Sister _____,
    We are happy your visit to _____
    Came when we celebrate Christ's birth,
    For it is His Star that we follow
    And it teaches "Peace on Earth."

    Your teachings of faith, courage and friendship
    Are the true spirit of Eastern Star,
    And we thank you again, our Silver Belle,
    For being the sweet person that you are.

A.M. *(comes forward with gift):*

Sister _____,
    You have heard the silver bells ringing

Our thanks and our happiness, too,
For they have been ringing merrily
Just to say that "We Love You."

Your friendship has been like a silver bell
Pure, and true, and so clear,
And mere words can never truly say
All the thanks that you should hear.

On behalf of _____ Chapter,
It is a pleasure to present to you
A Christmas Gift we hope you'll like
For it says again "We Love You."

NOTE: *When Guest is presented under Introductions at
first part of the meeting the following could be sung
to the old tune of* Silver Bell.

We bid you welcome, our Silver Belle
Under your spell
We've come to tell you of the love we are bringing
To wish you well
Happy to dwell, our Silver Belle.

MISCELLANEOUS

27. *Glory of God*
A Floral Ceremony
By Cornelia Schatmeyer, P.M.
(New Jersey)

⌐

MATRON:

That all things work together for the glory of those who love God, is nowhere more poignantly expressed than in a garden. There in the fresh turned earth, seeds are lovingly and faithfully planted and there they grow to fruition. From the wellsprings of heaven the rain falls to nurture the plants and the sun warms the earth to stimulate growth. Bees aid in the pollination of the plants and the excess of harmful insects is destroyed by the birds. Even the humble worm groveling beneath the earth serves its purpose by carrying valuable minerals to the surface. Eventually, the flowers come to bud and, in all their glory, burst into bloom. They are an inspiration to all and especially to that child, who, wandering in the garden, discovers his first flower. His wonder at the beauty that God has wrought is akin to pure worship. Oh, that we could all see God's glory with such purity of thought as is exhibited by children.

All things work to the glory of love,
And tonight we will bring to flower

The lessons which are seed for thought
In the teachings of the hour.

ASSOCIATE MATRON:

Once when the earth was drab and brown,
God caused the flowers to bloom,
Bringing us the glorious colors
Found in our Chapter room.

Through years they've been imitated
From the flowers we have seen
And we have copied for our own
Yellow, blue, white, red and green.

We emblazoned them upon our Star,
Enhanced with our lessons true,
Knowing the stories our colors suggest
Will always live on with you.

CONDUCTRESS:

You will now receive from our heroines, brave,
Floral reminders of the lectures they gave
To teach you the lessons you have heard,
Which we know you will cherish, word for word.

ASSOCIATE CONDUCTRESS:

And upon our altar so spotless white,
These tokens will be placed tonight
To be gathered together e'er we're through
Into a bouquet of colors for you.

ADAH:

Violets blue are my favorite flower,
And I place on the altar for you
The flower that should remind you
That you've taken a vow to be true.

RUTH:

> The jessamine is my favorite flower,
> It will urge you to always be kind
> And, in gathering of God's bounty,
> To keep the distressed in mind.

ESTHER:

> The lily is my favorite flower,
> Reminding you to serve, without fear,
> Any cause for good and honor,
> Knowing God is always near.

MARTHA:

> The fern is always my favorite,
> True faith it will symbolize,
> As in sorrow we turn to our Father,
> The more His strength to realize.

ELECTA:

> My favorite flower is the rose of red,
> To remind us from dawn to dark
> To keep our standard of charity high
> And always help to reach its mark.

MARSHAL:

> As you see me assemble these flowers
> Of colors varied and odd,
> So all things work together
> For the glory of those who love God.
>
> And once these blossoms are joined,
> Their colors and fragrance will blend
> And so they will serve to remind you
> That you'll be ever our sister and friend.

CHAPLAIN:

May we all work together in love,
Doing our best every day
To alleviate pain and sorrow
We may find upon life's way.

Replace each hatred with love,
Give kindness to wipe out pain,
And ever remember to thank
Our Father again and again.

God will increase our joy
As we demonstrate our love,
For He knows His own and sends them
His blessings from above.

28.   *Mothers Day Program*
By Ruth Adams, P.M.
(Arizona)

❧

Flower girls will have baskets of corsages for each mother.

W.M.:

Sisters and Brothers,
>   The dictionary defines the word "Mother"
>   As one who gives protective care,
>   And so, tonight, we honor our mothers
>   As our pride and our love we bear.

>   Mothers come in many sizes—
>   From a tiny nine to a large fifty-two,
>   Large or small—it makes no difference,
>   They watch over us in all we do.

>   Mothers come in different colors—
>   Brunettes, blonds and red heads, too,
>   And I'm happy there are mothers also
>   Whose hair is silvery-blue.

(Pin corsage on mother who is sitting in the East, providing she too is a P.M. Have other mothers presented at this time.)

ADAH:

My Sisters,
>   I represent the daughter's point
>   Which is the lovely color of blue.
>   Adah's lesson teaches that through our lives

We should strive to be faithful and true.
You've been guided by the open Bible
And have been true to honor and right,
So, tonight, we are pleased to greet you
With our love—and flowers sweet and bright.

(have mothers reseated)

ELECTA:

My Sisters,
 I represent the mother's point
 Which is the vibrant color of red.
 Electa's lesson teaches us loving kindness
 As the pathway of life we tread.

 We are proud to honor all of our mothers
 For the kindness you've shown every day;
 And it is now our special joy
 To present to you our love's bouquet.

(Flower girls give a corsage to each mother on the sidelines)

W.M.:

My Sisters,
 Mothers have a special place
 That no one else can fill,
 They gave us life, and our ideals,
 And, now and then, a pill.

 So let's give thanks for our mothers
 And their love through all the years,
 To sons, daughters and grandchildren, too,
 We love you mothers, and think you are dears.

Song:

> M is for the million things she gave me
> O means only that she's growing old,
> T is for the tears shed to save me
> H is for her heart of purest gold
> E is for her eyes with love-light shining
> R is for the right she'll always be
> Put them all together they spell mother
> A word that means the world to me.

29. *Ceremony for a Thanksgiving Program*
By Etta May Gibbany, P.M.
(Missouri)

⤵

Theme song: "America the Beautiful"

1. Formation at Star Points by girls in white formals.

2. Chaplain prays at the altar.

3. The First Thanksgiving.

4. Thanks for our Order, by extra girls at Star Point stations.

5. Choir sings one or more verses of theme song.

6. Retiring drill.

While the theme song is played as a march, twenty-five girls in white formals (or any number of girls available, but should be divisible by five) enter in single file, a few feet apart. If the number is sufficient, lines cross back of Esther's station, march down the sides of the room, outside the labyrinth, and form semi-circles around each Star Point. One of the girls at each Star Point station has the speaking part.

The music continues softly through the prayer, and through the speaking parts, if desired. The volume should be increased when the choir sings, and for the retiring march.

After the entrance drill, and formation of semi-circles at Star Point stations, the Chaplain walks slowly to the altar and kneels for prayer.

CHAPLAIN:

O God of love, whose tender care
Transcends all lands and creeds,
We pray that Thou wilt hear our prayer
Of praise, for all our needs.

We thank Thee for our own fair land,
For blessings manifold,
For landscapes painted by Thy hand
Rich hues, with autumn gold;

For bounteous harvest, fruit and grain
To feed a hungry world.
O, may true brotherhood remain
The Flag of Peace, unfurled,

Through Jesus Christ, our Lord, Amen.

WORTHY MATRON *(or a Reader):*

THE FIRST THANKSGIVING

The first Thanksgiving, we are told
Was by the saddened Pilgrim band
And followed death and winter's cold
For they had marched across the land.

But hope had come with summer's sun
And when they gathered in the corn
In sixteen hundred twenty-one,
Our own Thanksgiving Day was born.

The women, children, Indians, too,
With busy hands prepared the feast,
With songs of praise and prayers anew
Three days had passed before it ceased.

Now we have countless blessings more
For which we should have thankful hearts—
Our churches, homes and harvests' store,
And blessings each of these imparts.

SPEAKER AT ADAH'S STATION:

"THANKS FOR OUR ORDER"

I'm thankful for our Eastern Star
And Adah's ray of blue,
Its teachings reach to lands afar,
Its beauty, ever new.

SPEAKER AT RUTH'S STATION:

And I give thanks for the yellow ray
And for the lessons we have from Ruth,
Her faith and love shall well portray
To all eternal truth.

SPEAKER AT ESTHER'S STATION:

And Esther's ray of white, we know
Among our symbols, has a place,
It tells us in the long ago
She saved her people and her race.

SPEAKER AT MARTHA'S STATION:

And I give thanks for the ray of green
Which tells of Martha's trust,
A greater faith was never seen
When grief on her was thrust.

SPEAKER AT ELECTA'S STATION:

The ray of red, high in our ranks
Of symbols, is the mother's sign,
For this we should extend our thanks
To Him, our Lord, Divine!

CHOIR: "America the Beautiful" *(one or more verses, as time permits.)*

ORGANIST: *(plays the theme song as a march for the retiring drill.)*

30. Our Chapter Rainbow
To Honor Visiting Rainbow Girls
By Dorothy Trimble, P.M.
(Indiana)

This unique program features a small Rainbow in the East. Make this of cardboard about three feet long and seven inches high and cover it with rows of satin ribbon in the seven colors. Mount on a background of neutral gray, cut to follow the lines of the Rainbow, standing up about six inches higher. On this background place the seven colored letters spelling the word "Rainbow." Arrange letters same distance apart, evenly spaced, and when each color is explained, in verse, the speaker pins her rosette of ribbon in the appropriate color between the letters. Place the Rainbow on an easel in the East, at the foot of the dais in front of Worthy Matron's pedestal. It's very effective if a spotlight is played on it during the program.

———

Following the closing of the Chapter, the Worthy Matron announces that a Rainbow Program will be given. She calls up the Chapter and all sing:

Tune: "There's a Rainbow 'Round My Shoulder"

There's a Rainbow 'round our Chapter,
Lighting up our eastern sky;
With our Star bright, the Rainbow light
Makes shadows fly.

There's a Rainbow 'round our Chapter,
Worthy Matron wants it here;

She think it's Grand to lend a hand
　　To her project, dear.

There's a Rainbow 'round our Chapter
　　And it fits us like a glove;
Let the world have storm, we'll all be warm
　　In Fra-tern-al Love.

　　　　(Worthy Matron seats Chapter)

CONDUCTRESS:

Our Worthy Grand Matron told us
　　Of a project, her aim and dream;
When we began searching for it
　　It was in the Rainbow's gleam.

This interesting order was started
　　In the year Nineteen Twenty-two;
And our teen age Chapter daughters
　　Will enjoy this history, too.

As we listen to the members
　　Explain each color and glow,
We'll feel our hearts responding
　　To the appeal of the Rainbow.

(Electa, Chaplain, Ruth, Martha, Adah, Marshal and Esther now go up and stand in Rainbow formation behind the Easel, facing West. Each carries a small rosette of satin ribbon. Electa comes forward, explains her color, pins the nosegay between the letters and stands in front, a little to the left, still facing West, and one by one the others follow her, still keeping their Rainbow line:)

ELECTA:

> Vivid Red means intense LOVE,
> Solid, rich, enduring;
> First Rainbow color from above,
> His Love to us assuring.

CHAPLAIN:

> Burning RELIGION'S Orange flame
> Lights the steep path of duty,
> Teaches that work done in His Name
> Fills the humblest life with beauty.

RUTH:

> The golden glow of Rainbow Yellow
> Must be close to God's warm heart;
> Sunshine, flowers, sunsets mellow,
> In NATURE play the finest part.

MARTHA:

> IMMORTAL Green brings quiet peace,
> Thoughts of life, beyond the sun;
> Where all our fears will cease
> And a fuller life be begun.

ADAH:

> The heavenly Blue of God's sky
> Bids us be FAITHFUL and true;
> Leading from low ways to high
> With its message "Be True Blue."

MARSHAL:

> The INDIGO hue that will never fade
> > Colors each Patriot's creed;
> Loyal and brave we walk unafraid,
> > PATRIOTIC in word and deed.

ESTHER:

> When SERVICE we find in the Violet ray,
> > To the very least, our Brother,
> Then we are living the Rainbow Way,
> > In fraternal love with each other.

(Officers remain in this Rainbow formation as Worthy Matron calls up the Chapter and all sing):

TUNE: "An Old Spinning Wheel In The Parlor"

> Now a bright Rainbow shines on our Chapter,
> Bringing dreams to the young girls we love;
> Making each life worthwhile, filled with rapture,
> Brightened by God's Rainbow, up above.

> Sometime we'll see the colors' meaning very clearly,
> Shining in each act, and glowing in each deed;
> To their hearts the Rainbow held so dearly,
> Lights the way for those troubled, in need.

Clippings

Clippings

Clippings

Clippings

Clippings